101 LESSONS FROM THE SKY

FLETCHER MCKENZIE

SSP

First Edition

ISBN 978-0-473-44883-7 (Paperback edition)
ISBN 978-0-473-44884-4 (Mobi edition)

Published by Squabbling Sparrows Press
PO Box 26 126, Epsom, Auckland 1023
New Zealand

CONTENTS

"By far the greater number of aeroplane accidents are due to precisely the same circumstances that have caused previous accidents. A distressing feature of these accidents is the evidence they afford of the unwillingness, or the inability, of many pilots to profit from the experiences and mistakes of others."

Gustav Hamel and Charles C. Turner
Flying: Some Practical Experiences
Published posthumously in 1914

LESSONS FROM THE SKY

NEAR MISSES & STORIES FROM
101 AIR TRANSPORT PILOTS
IN AUSTRALIA, USA AND THE UNITED KINGDOM

I dedicate this book to Richard Bach. His book Johnathon Livingston Seagull had a huge impact on my life, and his short story books helped me understand that life is full of stories which makes us who we are. Richard responded to my first email with "Fletch Lives", and he even enjoyed our TV show FlightPathTV.

Thank you to Carlo Santoro, who helped me understand and enjoy the intricate differences of commercial aviation. Over a decade of a journey of countless hours of flying and working together Carlo helped me see the passion of how many people love this industry.

To all the professional and commercial pilots who followed their dream to fly, to spend their lives above the earth constantly fighting gravity. I look forward to meeting you one day.

FOREWORD

ADAM ELTHAM

"A superior pilot uses his superior judgement to avoid situations
which require the use of his superior skill"
Frank Borman
NASA Astronaut

This quote along with fellow astronaut John Young's response to the
question of whether he was a little nervous about the first space
shuttle mission, strike a humorous, and perhaps sarcastic, reality
check that this profession is for keeps. And if you have no understanding or appreciation of the risks and how to best manage them,
you may need more than superior skill.

Many people ask whether we do much in the cockpit these days
so I begin explaining the dynamics of risk mitigation and how on a
daily basis that's a large driver dictating how we operate. I like to
point out that commercial aviation has plenty of competition out
there when it comes to operating environments that have extreme
consequences if these risks are not anticipated.

Having read about the ill fated Piper Alpha, the environmental
tragedy of Love Canal in Niagara, Three Mile Island, and Chal-

lenger serve as a reminder of how events can go terribly wrong, very quickly.

For those of us not necessarily blessed with these superior skills, systems have been developed over time from many less fortunate before us which assist in enhancing judgement and decision making in the form of Standard Operating Procedures (SOP's), Quick Reference Handbooks (QRH's), and Checklists.

These procedures, references and checklists provide risk mitigating steps in the ever increasing human machine automated interface because as it turns out, us humans are quite adept in the art of inadvertently inducing mistakes, whether deliberate or not, through distraction or fatigue, and while may appear harmless enough at the time, ultimately have the potential to kick a catastrophic chain of events into motion.

Aside from the critical processes that are developed and implemented, as individuals we can accelerate those learnings by talking about those awkward moments in our careers where things haven't gone so well. Unfortunately though, it doesn't seem that easy...

Many find it undesirable to share their experiences. Is it because of fear of shame, appearing weak or even ego related? Have you ever said sorry to your partner? Probably ranks up there with the same difficulty!

Fletcher's book *81 Lessons From The Sky*, reminds you that you are very much NOT alone. *101 Lessons From The Sky* should reassure you that it doesn't matter where you are in the food chain, we all have valuable lessons to learn from each other.

The more stories I read, the more stories I hear, the more experience I gained, have all improved my awareness and understanding of the risks.

I have known Fletcher since he took some excellent footage in one of my finest hours towing banners for his TV show *FlightPathTV*. Turns out my wife knew him from way back but didn't recognise him with his clothes on (standard swimmers joke).

As upwardly mobile chaps since that meeting, we have both

managed the risks associated with aviation and despite only flying together on rare occasions, the flights have been quite the adventure. Our families and friends know all about our individual stories, which at times have been shared with the regulatory authorities to assist in their findings for pilots that sadly no longer have a voice of their own.

Fletcher continues to embrace these stories at a commercial level by further challenging the benefits and importance of getting that message out there.

If you're sitting on the fence, I once read "if you have the ability, then you have the responsibility". Adopting this thought process hopefully moulds a culture to ensure you consider safety first, and to share your story even if it comes from an inadvertent error, mistake or oversight. Everyone should be striving to achieve a "just culture" within themselves and their organisations.

When I entered the next stage of my career as part of a two pilot crew in the commercial world with my Air Transport Pilot Licence, I discovered it created a renewed environment to begin the next level of mistakes and oversights.

Commencing my first jet rating on the 737 Classic, my sim buddy and I discovered regularly that we were both making identical mistakes with the new level of automation almost on a daily basis along with the odd random act of madness. This sharing of perceived inadequacies served as an incredibly powerful tool to accelerate our learning, alleviate huge amounts of stress and believe it or not, boost confidence. We still compare our short fallings on a regular basis today and despite now working in different companies, and now on the 737NG, we still come up with unintentionally inventive ways to load up the Captain.

Reducing the speed dial instead of turning the heading bug on climb out given their co location on the automation panel, the quartering tailwind on landing, initially experiencing a go around in atrocious weather, going with flight planned fuel instead of having some extra up your sleeve when *Murphy* steps in and incidents where the automation decides to disengage, requiring immediate reverting to hands-on flying on approach are just a few examples of what would otherwise be a smooth procedural experience turned very quickly into a heightened state of awareness.

Reading Ernest Gann's *Fate is the Hunter* helped me understand that these mistakes have been going on for ever and a day when taking that next step up.

I have always found stories retold by humble, approachable and credible aviators provided the greatest reassurance that your short fallings are not always unique.

In my experience, the pilot you speak to who has *no* stories to share, is the one you need to be aware of.

The best example I have seen of how you can level the playing field in what can at times be a highly stressful working environment where there are numerous degrees of experience was in my past life as a Police Officer. One of the team was responsible for carrying THE notebook for a five week cycle and any random acts of foolery from ANY member (bosses not excluded) were appropriately reported on. At the end of this cycle, the team gathered and these stories were unleashed. Let's just say, I featured regularly. Those shared stories may have been on the light-hearted side, but looking back on them, each was a lesson for the rest of the team, shared with the team, in a safe team environment.

Adam Eltham
Pilot

Born into aviation while his father was a ground engineer with BOAC and British Caledonian, Adam spent 14 years with the New Zealand Police including a deployment to the Solomon Islands, and ended his time as a Detective with the Special Investigation Group. He completed a handful of Air Safety Investigation Papers under the late Ron Chippendale who introduced him to the New Zealand Society of Air Safety Investigators (NZSASI).

Adam continued instruction to Multi Engine B-Category level including Aerobatics, Tail wheel, Banner Towing, holds a New Zealand and Australian ATPL and is rated on numerous single and light twins including 1947 Miles Messenger, Harvard and DC3 to the Boeing 737 Classic and NG.

He is currently operating the 737NG around the South Pacific and Tasman along with representing his current company as a Brand Ambassador and serving on the Recruitment Panel.

INTRODUCTION

CONNELL WESTON

After learning to fly at Ardmore Airport, in Auckland, my first job was as an flight instructor at the North Shore Aero Club.

Following the demise of the F27 with Air New Zealand, many highly qualified airline pilots were laid off, flooding the GA market leaving no jobs for a career progression. As a consequence, myself and a good friend travelled to Zimbabwe to take up employment with in Harare.

Harare was where I clocked up just over 1000hrs flying Barons, Cessna 401, Britten Norman Islander and Piper Aztec - all highly sort after multi hours.

Next stop was Botswana, to the Okavango to fly a variety of Cessna singles and twins including the C208, Caravan.

Followed by a stint in South Africa flying out of Johannesburg's Lanseria, where I got to fly a Beechcraft King Air.

After four years away from New Zealand, it was time to come home, where I worked for a Wellington based company, flying across the Cook Strait to the Marlborough Sounds.

An Air New Zealand feeder airline based in Gisborne was next.

To take advantage of Asia's amazing flying opportunities, I moved to Malaysia to fly Metroliners for a start-up, which unfortunately didn't last long.

Where one door closes another opens, it certainly helps to be the Johnny-on-the-spot! My jet flying career had started with the B737-200 freighter, working for a Malaysian company in Jakarta.

Plenty of potential job opportunities become available for a pilot with jet time.

August 1999 saw a move Hong Kong where I gained most of my Airbus experience, becoming an examiner on both the A320 and A330, albeit not at the same time.

And then a brief stint with an LCC (low cost carrier) based in Christchurch, New Zealand. And this is where my story begins...

It was to be just another takeoff... yes we were a little heavy, carrying fuel for a 3hr sector, 1.2ohr alternate and all the company reserves.

The ATIS has passing showers, mid 20kts wind from the left about 30 degrees off the vector.

15 years flying both the Airbus A320 and the A330, and the machines had never skipped a beat!

Until today...

I call V1, rotate is about 10-12kts more, wet runway and all.

Somewhere between "V1" and "rotate" there was a deafening popping and banging sound coming from the left side of the plane.

Somehow I managed to squeak out "rotate".

I glanced at EWD, engine warning display. ENG 1 EGT OVERLIMIT. Couldn't help noticing the digital readout of the EGT was RED with the numbers steadily increasing through 900 odd degrees.

It wasn't my sector but my trusty first officer was doing a cracking job, but I still had to make sure "mate have you got this?" My first error!

In the commercial airline world we are so versed on SOPs, standard calls with cue based communication. Instead of positive climb which should've been the first words uttered from me, I said "mate have you got this"

After taming the angry beast on the left, by simple retarding the thrust lever, we recognised the gear was still hanging-out at around 1000 ft agl.

It wasn't the stock standard engine failure practiced in the simulator. In the sim the engine would normally catch on fire, sustain obvious damage with $N1$ seizing and instant loss of thrust. A basic flame out requiring a restart once safe to do so.

In our situation, when the thrust lever was bought back to idle, all the bad disappeared.

Although both engines were running, only one was keeping us in the sky. We kept the faulty motor running at idle to utilise the primary source of the Green hydraulic system and electrics.

After calculating landing distance required for our weight, it was quickly determined that returning to the GC was out of the question. With the assistance of engineering we decided to divert to Brisbane. Longer runway, good engineering and a much better chance of finding a solution to get the passengers across the Tasman Sea.

In the wash up it was determined that the effect of "startle factor" is significant and compelling. There were a few other safety recommendations handed down, which of course have all been taken on.

After all my years of flying in countless aircraft of every type, and even now as a contract captain with a Chinese carrier, there hasn't been a single incident I haven't learnt from, no matter how small, or like in the story above, how big.

Never stop learning from the experiences of others, including mine.

Connell Weston
Pilot

A pilot for over 30 years, flying everything from a Piper Cub to an Airbus 330, with extensive experience in New Zealand in both GA, instructing and airline operations.

Connell enjoyed four years flying around Southern Africa during his youth flying high performance turbine powered twins, and many years flying an Airbus out of Hong Kong. He is now a contract pilot for a Chinese airline.

PROLOGUE

"Most accidents originate in actions committed by reasonable, rational individuals who were acting to achieve an assigned task in what they perceived to be a responsible and professional manner."
Peter Harle
Director of Accident Prevention
Transportation Safety Board of Canada
(And former RCAF pilot)

LEARNING FROM AVIATION EXPERIENCES

FLETCHER MCKENZIE

Unlike the oceans, which only cover 71% of the world, the sky covers the entire globe, regardless of where you are.

Since prehistoric times, birds have flown through our skies, and as soon as humankind walked the earth, men and women, dreamers and visionaries, imagined flying effortlessly like those birds.

Before history's first recorded flight, Leonardo da Vinci probably came the closest to understanding the form of flight. He studied, drew and dissected birds to understand the mechanics of flight. Leonardo designed complex flying machines, which were discovered years after his death, but to date no evidence has been unearthed to categorically document that he flew in one of his machines.

Since the Montgolfier brothers launched a balloon on a tether with Jean-François Pilâtre de Rozier in 1783, people have been able to soar with the birds. Those early aviators learnt lessons from their experiences - lessons which have been documented and passed on to future aviators. Some religiously, some not so much.

I remember one of my first hard hitting learnings, from my nineteenth parachute jump. I had worked my way up from static to free fall and was now jumping at 14,500 feet with a dive exit from a

Cessna 402. I was doing around a one minute free fall and it was awesome.

Disappointingly, before that jump, it was a little windy, so I had a chat with the jump master – who said that the wind was pushing the limits of my chute. My heart sunk, but I was so keen, so it was suggested I pack my chute and then we could make a call closer to the time. Good idea... and off I went.

I did my usual briefing and packed my chute slowly and methodically, and after fifteen minutes I was ready for approval from one of the jump masters. Signed off!

When it came time to make a call, it was a simple yes, but I was to jump out second to last. The jump master was concentrating on the free fall guy. I was confident as to what I had to do. With the usual load we entered the 402, sat on our bums and shuffled into each other (no seats). We climbed into the heavens to jump out of a perfectly good aircraft. Then it came - door open, check the wind, check position, 30 second call, power off, and go. Out we went, some as a group, and then me by myself. That was the easy part.

As I exited the aircraft, adrenaline and excitement pumped through my body. The freezing slip stream hitting my face as I accelerated towards the ground. The first 1000 feet is covered in 12 seconds, increasing until I'm hitting 6 seconds per 1000 feet. Then I start my exercises with a few flips, tracking across the sky, not thinking about where I am...

I was downwind of the landing zone. The airfield is a big field - an active air force base for large jet aircraft. However I was well north of the airfield, over a residential area.

I complete a number of flips and turn practice, and stare at the ground and see it getting bigger and bigger. A good 60 seconds of free fall, and I still don't realise exactly where I am in relation to the wind.

Finally I checked my altimeter, gave it a few more seconds and pull my rip cord at around 3000 feet, and prepare for the extreme braking.

Boom. The explosion rips through my legs as the leg straps take my weight, braking like a car. I look up and see what I need to see - a full flying chute. I grab my straps and try turning left and right. All good.

Only now do I start looking for the landing zone. I seem to be a fair away from the airfield. No problem, I will fly towards the field, but after ten seconds I realise I am not making the headway I should. I am almost over a creek and realise I won't be making the landing zone today, and start hoping that I will make the field. Hope is not a good strategy.

I am hanging almost falling vertically down, instead of the usual 20 knots air speed, I was not moving. I play this over and over in my mind. I jumped too early, I never checked that I was downwind of the landing zone, I never had to check this before, the wind was 15-20 knots, my airspeed of my chute was 20 knots.

I started looking for a drop zone amongst the glasshouses and tall trees used to shelter the neighbouring orchards.

At around 500 feet I feel I am making some progress, believing that there is less wind closer to the ground, giving me a glimmer of hope, until I saw the power lines and fences topped with barbed wire. I was trying to determine whether my angle and speed would get me over the obstacles or whether I'd be cooked on the cables. I decided trying was a bad idea, remembering my instructor's advice of 'if you think you are going to hit something, turn away'. So I did.

I'd spotted a small open area between a shelter-belt of trees and decided to head for that. I turned downwind, and my groundspeed went from a few knots to nearly 40 knots. I thought I had better turn early to bleed my speed back to a few knots... too easy. As I was 100-50 feet above the ground, the wind had decreased and now I had my 20 knots and the shelter-belt was looming up in front of me. I'd been told to turn, so I did.

The ground was rushing up towards me and things were flashing past in a blur. I don't remember a lot of what happened next, but I remember trying to flare.

I hit the ground hard, with the wind knocked out of me and pain shooting through my body. I remember fighting to breathe with a sharp pain in my chest. I could hear shouting but couldn't see, my vision totally gone despite my eyes being open. I was however, alive.

That's what you call a close call.

As the oxygen returned to my lungs, my neck and ankle started throbbing, together with a sharp pain in my side every time I took a breath. Foolishly I realise I'm still wearing my googles which are caked in mud. I'd landed in thick, sticky mud - in a pig sty. Mud, which cushioned my landing and covered my googles, thereby obscuring my sight.

After removing the mud-covered googles, I saw the glass house only a few meters away - a very close call. Landing there would have had a very different ending.

My club mates find me, check me over, grab the chute, and I limp into the rescue car. One of the jump masters thinks I may have broken a rib, so I head off to A&E (the Accident & Emergency Clinic). The doctor diagnoses a bruised liver.

A week later, despite still being in severe pain, I attended a toga party, which may have involved drinking half a bottle of Ouzo... I started vomiting, and didn't stop - back to A&E, where it turns out I have internal bleeding.

Turns out that on impact, my liver went through my ribcage, lacerating my liver - a bit like putting a sheet of paste through a spaghetti machine. No drinking alcohol for the next six months, and weekly check ups.

My learnings - when jumping out of a plane, the first thing to do is establish my position and where I am in relation to the airfield and the wind, and to get myself into the upwind position by tracking across the sky.

An expensive and painful experience, but one I walked away from. Others have not been so lucky.

The word Aviation originates from the Latin word *Avis*, meaning bird. It is a noun, meaning of; the design, development, production, operation, and use of aircraft, especially heavier-than-air aircraft.

Aviation developed quickly. In just over a hundred years it progressed from only being able to glide with the wind, to being able to reach the stars with the invention of powered flight. That it developed at all is due in part to the amazing story of two bicycle-shop owning brothers - Orville and Wilbur Wright, who, on the sand dunes of Kill Devils Hill, four miles south of the town Kittyhawk, achieved the impossible over the very well funded Samuel Langley - the recipient of a War Department grant of $50,000, and $20,000 from the Smithsonian, to develop a piloted airplane. But it was the Wright brothers 'Flying Machine' which was the first powered airplane to execute controlled and sustained flight.

There are other first flight claims made by Clément Ader, Gustave Whitehead, Richard Pearse, and Karl Jatho for their variously documented tests in the years prior to and including 1903. Claims that the first true flight occurred after 1903 are made by Traian Vuia and Alberto Santos-Dumont. Controversy surrounds published accounts and Whitehead's own claims that he flew a powered machine successfully several times in 1901 and 1902.

Sadly a huge number of accidents have shaped the global aviation industry, but almost all of them have made the world of air transport safer.

I have picked out a handful of Air Transport accidents that I have a strong link with, and which I believe the majority of traveling passengers would understand and recognise straight away when they hear of the changes to safety heralded by those incidents.

This is the key outcome I want to achieve with this book, the changes we make, the lessons we learn from the mishaps of others, or the experiences we take note of to ensure we don't make the same mistake.

Please read this book with the intent of making notes and seeing what habits you could look at building, changing or eliminating.

As a New Zealander, I enjoy the thought that Richard Pearse, in his flying exploits deep in the South Island near Timaru, may have in fact beaten the Wright Brothers. We will never know for sure. An experienced team of engineers and pilots are building a replica of his plane and attempting to fly it in New Zealand. Interesting enough Pearse himself, in the form of a letter he wrote to local newspapers in 1915, said:

> "The honour of inventing the aeroplane [...] is the product of many minds [but] pre-eminence will undoubtedly be given to the Wright brothers [...] as they were actually the first to make successful flights with a motor-driven aeroplane".

There were verified eyewitnesses who describe that during those attempts he would have reached at least three meters high and had a flight of several hundred meters - and that on two seperate occasions he crashed into a hedge. He did learn from setbacks and kept flying and working away at constructing a tilt-rotor flying-machine for personal use for driving on the road, as well as for flying. If only he could see what the world was experimenting with now.

The first aviation passenger death was on Sept 17 1908, during flight trials to win a contract from the Army Signal Corps, in a plane piloted by Orville Wright. Orville made 15 flights at Fort Myer, setting three world records on September 9th, including a 62-minute flight and the first public passenger flight. One of the wooden propellor blades spilt and hit bracing wire, flicking the rear rudder from vertical to horizontal causing the aircraft to pitch nose down and crash. Orville was injured, the passenger - 26 year old Lieutenant Thomas Selfridge, suffered a fractured skull, dying hours later. The Army was still impressed, and in July 1909 they awarded the contract to the Wright bothers. But one lesson learnt from that crash was Army pilots were required to wear helmets in order to minimise head injuries. Orville Wright began training pilots in March 1910, at the The Wright Flying School, training 119 students to fly Wright airplanes.

Further aviation advances were made through the drive for innovation from the military sector. WWI was the first military conflict where aviation made massive leaps in design and performance. At the start of WWI aircraft were not considered as a serious tool of war - they were used for upsetting reconnaissance balloons which were being used for artillery spotting. Germany employed Zeppelins for reconnaissance over the North Sea and Baltic and also for strategic bombing raids over Britain and the Eastern Front.

The impact of aircraft on the course of WWI was more tactical than strategic, most important being direct cooperation with ground forces (especially for ranging and correcting artillery fire).

Aircraft soon replaced balloons and would venture out on reconnaissance missions, photographing the opposition's troop positions and movements. They carried foot spikes and other weapons to throw from their aircraft to support their own troops in the ground war below.

Early WWI stories record pilots and crew of opposing aircraft exchanging a friendly wave or two. This soon changed to throwing grenades, grappling hooks and other items. On 8 September 1914, the first aircraft brought down by another was an Austrian reconnaissance aircraft rammed by Russian pilot Pyotr Nesterov in the Eastern Front. The aircraft crashed killing all of the occupants. This then progressed to pilots firing handheld firearms at enemy aircraft, however pistols were too inaccurate and the single shot rifles too unlikely to score a hit.

I helped film 'World War One Top Gun Revealed', in Masterton,

New Zealand. An hour long programme, produced in 2012 in association with the Bedlam Productions UK (the producers of the movie The King's Speech), with the amazing aircraft collection of Sir Peter Jackson at The Vintage Aviator Limited. The documentary charted the developments in reconnaissance, photography, firepower and speed. With amazing reproductions of the original aircraft, a B.E.2 and B.E.2c, we were able to demonstrate how hard it would have been to shoot from one aircraft to another, using a crew member with a laser rifle and laser tag sensors. Dealing with the slipstream, castor oil and looking out for the propellor, struts and wires, it was almost impossible.

When French pilot Louis Quenault opened fire on a German aircraft on October 5th 1914, with a machine gun, warfare would never be the same. A new era of air combat had begun.

New Zealand aviation was at the forefront of this burgeoning industry, thanks to brothers Leo and Vivian Walsh who built a British Howard Wright biplane to fly the first officially-recorded flight in New Zealand in early 1911 and went onto train 107 pilots for WWI.

The New Zealand Flying School in Mission Bay, Auckland was the first to be opened in October 1915 by the brothers, constructing several flying boats. The stone Melanesian Mission Building was used as the school's headquarters, and still stands today. They imported the first two Boeing aircraft outside of the United States and initiated airmail services, teaching many men to fly. Their actions helped a significant number pilots who went onto becoming great aviation pioneers themselves.

The first regular scheduled passenger service in New Zealand belongs to F. Maurice Clarke and Squadron-Leader Malcolm McGregor who started the airline 'Air Travel'. They launched a tri-weekly passenger service between Christchurch and Dunedin on November 6th 1930 with a De Havilland DH50 borrowed from the government. Sadly, passenger numbers were low and, and after nine months it closed down. Seven weeks later 'Dominion Airlines Ltd' began a daily service between Gisborne and Hastings, becoming the link between New Zealand and the areas ravaged by the Hawke's Bay earthquake. Just after the earthquake, after dropping a bag of telegrams in a field, the Desoutter II monoplane's engine stalled and the aircraft nosed-dived into the ground, killing the pilot and two passengers forcing 'Dominion Airlines' into liquidation. This was the first fatal air service accident in New Zealand.

In 1935 Boeing was competing against Douglas and Martin for a contract to build 200 bombers. The Boeing Model 299, 'X13372', outperformed both competitors and exceeded the air corps' performance specifications. It could fly further, faster, and carry more payload than either of the other two entries. On October 30th during one of the trials, two experienced Army pilots were at the controls of the Model 299. Major Ployer Peter Hill (his first time flying the 299) sat in the left seat with Lieutenant Donald Putt (the primary Army pilot for the previous evaluation flights) as the copilot. With them was Leslie Tower (the Boeing Chief Test Pilot), C.W. Benton (a Boeing mechanic), and Henry Igo (a representative of Pratt and Whitney, the engine manufacturer). It began to climb but suddenly stalled, crashing during take-off due to locked control surfaces, killing two of the five occupants, Major Hill, the U.S. Army Air Corps' Chief of Flight Testing and Leslie Tower.

The investigation by Boeing determined the pilots made an error by not unlocking the wind gust-lock. The gust-lock, one of the new features added, is engaged while on the ground to prevent elevator damage from high-wind situations, but must be released prior to take-off. As the pilot had to tend to all four engines while monitoring a huge number of new buttons, levers and gauges, the pilot had forgotten to release the new locking mechanism on the elevator and rudder controls. When the Model 299 took off with the gust-lock engaged the elevators were inoperable. Once airborne, Leslie Tower realised what was happening and tried to reach the lock handle but by that time it was too late.

Douglas won the competition and received an order for 133 of the DB-1 (based on the DC-2). The Air Corps gave Boeing a chance to keep the Model 299 alive with an additional 13 aircraft being ordered for further testing, closely watched by Boeing, Congress, and the War Department. Various articles state that the pilots sat down and put their heads together, and Boeing states it was Boeing experts, but either way, what resulted was a series of checklists, with four checklists developed:

1. Takeoff
2. Flight
3. Before landing
4. After landing

The Model 299 was not too difficult for one man to fly, it was simply too complex for one man's memory. The checklists for both the pilot and the co-pilot made sure that nothing was missed, especially unlocking the wind gust-lock. Of course now known as the control check - full and free movement - the last check pilots must do before take off.

The 299 was introduced to the Army Corps in 1938 as the B-17 Flying Fortress. This aircraft evolved through numerous design advances, becoming the third-most produced bomber, with 12,731 aircraft produced.

World War II pushed aviation design and technology even further, jumping ahead at a dizzying pace, the first turbojet aircraft to fly was the Heinkel He 178 V1 in 1939 and the first operational turbojet aircraft, the Messerschmitt Me 262 was pressed into service by the German Luftwaffe in April 1944, the same year the British followed with their jet - the Gloster Meteor, it was committed to defence of the UK flying against the V-1 buzz bomb or *doodlebug*. The civil sector benefited from these huge military advances. However with such advances in technology there were errors, mistakes and losses - many lessons have been learnt from aircraft crashing, the cost was people ultimately losing their lives.

Then came the jet age, the first purpose-built jet airliner was the

British de Havilland Comet which first flew in 1949 and entered service in 1952. Also developed in 1949 was the Avro Canada C102 Jetliner, which never was produced; however the term jetliner became a generic term for passenger jet aircraft. Within a year problems started to emerge, three Comets lost within 12 months in highly publicised accidents, after suffering catastrophic in-flight break-ups. Two of the accidents were found to be caused by structural failure resulting from metal fatigue in the airframe, a phenomenon not fully understood at the time. So the Comet was extensively redesigned, with oval windows, structural reinforcements and other changes. Rival manufacturers meanwhile heeded the lessons learned from the Comet while developing their own aircraft. The Comet was adapted for a variety of military roles including a specialised maritime patrol variant, the Hawker Siddeley Nimrod, which remained in service with the Royal Air Force until 2011.

Aviation has been the main industry able to learn from its mistakes and it learned fast, evolving with new procedures, training processes and checklists. The crash investigation process became more and more professional.

Air travel has flourished everywhere, in New Zealand we have a flightless bird as our National icon, but New Zealand's aviation industry has grown over the years with a disproportionately high number of aviation entrepreneurs, aircraft designers, new airlines and air services and a large agricultural air industry. Fuelled by an urge to overcome our isolation between towns and the rest of the world. New Zealand has had its share of air accidents, some lucky escapes and some not so lucky. Due to this isolation and remoteness, New Zealand still has 17 aircraft still missing and unaccounted for.

My father worked in the National Airways Corporation (NAC) office in Auckland. I was recently given one of my fathers pay slips by my mother (In April 1978 the NAC merged with Air New Zealand).

I fondly remember that whenever we drove to Tauranga or past the Kaimai Ranges to Matamata he would tell us about the NAC Flight 441 DC-3 which crashed into the Kaimai Ranges and how he knew one of the flight attendants onboard. I still have his DC-3 model he made for the office, hand painted in the NAC colours. I always wondered how and why Flight 441 had crashed, and it wasn't until years later when I read Rev. Dr. Richard Waugh's book, "The Kaimai Crash: New Zealand's Worst Air Crash" on the accident and recovery that I understood what had happened.

New Zealand's Civil Aviation Authority's (CAA) investigation pointed to a strong downdraft that pushed the aircraft below the ranges, and in poor weather conditions the aircraft encountered extreme turbulence which the crew and aircraft were unable to recover from. Another aircraft the same day was also caught but managed to recover. The CAA made the following changes as a result of the crash, marking the Kaimai Ranges as mountainous terrain, and raising the minimum safe altitude by 1000 feet.

I grew up on the Bucklands Beach peninsula in Auckland and often frequented Musick Point, usually to search for frogs in the creek and to swim off the rocks at the tip of the point. It was named in 1942 after Pan-American Clipper Captain Edwin Musick who collected 10 world records for seaplanes, holding more flying records than any other pilot, Captain Musick reportedly flew two million trans-ocean miles in airline service. He and his crew of six died in the crash of a Sikorsky S-42 flying boat on an inaugural flight from the United States to New Zealand. After reporting an engine oil leak one hour after take-off from Pago Pago, Samoa, they turned back. Too heavy to land safely, the crew dumped fuel in preparation for landing, and an explosion occurred. Pan American believed that the fuel dump values were too close to the engine exhaust ports and the vaporised fuel and heat caused the explosion.

Memories of an air crash I remember as a child was the news on November 28th 1979 when flight TE901, an Air New Zealand McDonnell Douglas DC-10-30, went missing. I remember a comment being made regarding flight times, stating that at the time all fuel would have been exhausted and the details that a rescue operation to find the aircraft had been started. I remember my seven year old thought process lead me to believe that maybe it landed somewhere, or they were in life rafts and the radio just didn't work - I had hope. Sadly this was not the case.

To understand why the seven-year-old me had such hope, the adult me found the following statement online:

"The aircraft has extensive life support systems on board, in the way of rafts, vests.... ....we would like to say that there is still some hope that passengers may be alive"
Craig Saxon
Air New Zealand's Public Affairs Director
(He went on to mention that Air New Zealand's chief executive Morrie Davis comments also expressed earlier that there is still considerable hope.)

Air New Zealand Flight 901 (TE-901) (TE was the Airline (IATA) code for Tasman Empire Airways Limited (TEAL), the forerunner of Air New Zealand - TE was used for international flights and NZ for domestic flights until 1990). Flight 901 was the fourteenth scheduled Air New Zealand Antarctic sightseeing flight that operated between 1977 and 1979. The aircraft would leave Auckland in the morning, fly a number of hours sightseeing over the Antarctic, then return to Auckland in the evening after a refuelling stop in Christchurch.

On November 28th 1979, flight TE-901, registration ZK-NZP, crashed into Mount Erebus on Ross Island, Antarctica, killing all 237 passengers and 20 crew on board.

It was then the fourth biggest air disaster in the world and New Zealand's deadliest peacetime disaster, and still the biggest air disaster involving a New Zealand-owned aircraft. An air crash which has haunted New Zealander's and families globally.

With only a small population of only three million, the loss and horror hit New Zealand hard - almost everybody knew or had some association with somebody among the victims.

For weeks and months I remember Mum and Dad watching the news and I remember seeing the images of the aircraft remains strewn along the mountain side of Mt Erebus in Antartica. The country was in grief, so many questions, so many fingers pointed. Then the stories around the people who tragically died onboard starting being published. Also published were the many errors which were made and a chilling cover up by staff within Air New Zealand. Most disturbingly was the fact that people destroyed evidence to lay blame on the crew.

New Zealand's Chief Inspector of Air Accidents, Ron Chippendale, made his report to the public in May 1980, his report summarised that Captain Jim Collins had erred when the crew were unsure of their actual position but he continued on anyway - the crash was blamed on pilot error. The report did not criticise the airline other than a few small mistakes in the morning briefing. The term *polar whiteout* was defined as a leading suspect. However, with the increase of litigation with dependants claims and a very large public uneasiness, the New Zealand government decided to set up a Royal Commission, also in part to appease the New Zealand Air Line Pilots' Association investigating team and understand the areas of blame. It set out to understand what caused the crash and who, if anyone, was to blame. One man, a fellow pilot, Gordon Vette challenged this finding. He had trained Collins himself and found it unlikely that he would exhibit that level of negligence.

The commission, presided over by Justice Peter Mahon QC, concluded that the accident was caused by a correction made to the coordinates of the flight path the night before the disaster, coupled with a failure to inform the flight crew of the change, with the result that the aircraft, instead of being directed by computer down to McMurdo Sound (as the crew had been led to believe), was instead re-routed into the path of Mount Erebus. Justice Mahon's report accused Air New Zealand of presenting *'an orchestrated litany of lies'* and this led to changes in senior management at the airline.

The blame was not on the aircrew but indeed on Air New Zealand personnel in the Flight Operations Division, as they altered the latitudinal and longitudinal co ordinates of the waypoint without the aircrews knowledge. This was never communicated to the crew.

What were the lessons from this tragic accident?

Mahon's final report was published on April 27th 1981, and it largely agreed with Vette's hypotheses. Mahon found Air New Zealand to be financially responsible, describing their attempts to shift the blame on to the late flight crew as 'very clearly part of an attempt to conceal a series of disastrous administrative blunders'.

Vette's findings on the crash of Flight TE-901 were highly influential in advancing air safety and accident prevention in general. In an interview, Mahon said:

> "An overseas expert in jet training and jet operations has said that this report has made the world a safer place to fly in. Well if that is so, that is due to the persistence of Gordon Vette and the evidence he produced which directed me and counsel of the Royal Commission onto the right path."

Vette introduced the concepts of 'human factors' and 'organizational accidents' into the language of accident analysis and prevention.

I remember studying for Human Factors which included the many details of the Erebus crash, to understand how visual illusions play tricks on our minds - our brains making us see what we want to see.

Aviation Medicine and other Human Factors was one the most interesting books I had read in years. As I read deeper into the various close call reports, I wanted to understand the situations that the pilots got into, so I could understand what factors lead to poor decision making. I have made a few myself, seeing things I wanted to believe. These terms are still in use today as important considerations in airline safety. The International Civil Aviation Organisation (ICAO) used Vette's report as an example of how a combination of organisational failures could cause an accident, calling it '10 years ahead of its time' and adding that if these lessons had been followed, 'Chernobyl, Bhopal, Clapham Junction, King's Cross and certainly the Dryden Report would not have existed'.

Vette also recommended necessary instrumental improvements. He was also one of the first to suggest adding forward-looking capabilities to the Ground Proximity Warning System (GPWS), as the crew of Flight TE-901 only had six seconds to react before impacting with Mount Erebus. These recommendations became a factor in the development of Enhanced Ground Proximity Warning Systems (EGPWS) in the 1990's and Terrain Awareness and Warning System (TAWS) with forward-looking capabilities - TAWS systems are widely recommended by international airline safety organisations such as the United States Federal Aviation Administration (FAA), and TAWS systems have been installed in 95% of commercial jets by 2007.

On June 2nd 1983, a Canada Air McDonnell Douglas DC-9-32 Flight 797 was operating as an international passenger flight. Flying from Dallas/Fort Worth International Airport to Montréal–Dorval International Airport, the aircraft developed an in-flight fire behind the lavatory, it spread between the outer skin and the inner decor panels, filling the plane with toxic smoke. The fire burned through crucial electrical cables knocking out most of the instrumentation in the cockpit forcing the plane to divert. Within ninety seconds of landing the doors were open but sadly the fresh oxygen created a flashover (like a backdraft) combining heat and fuel and the interior became engulfed in flames killing 23 passengers which had not evacuated the aircraft.

The lessons from this accident contributed to changes to global regulations making aircraft travel safer. There were new requirements and new standards across the industry. Smoke detectors were installed in lavatories, new lighting to mark pathways to exit doors, and delivering firefighting training to flight crews with new firefighting equipment onboard. Passengers seated in an over-wing exit row are now instructed to assist in an emergency, and it became mandatory for aircraft manufacturers to prove evacuation could be done in 90 seconds.

In 2017, 4.1 billion travellers flew safely on 41.8 million flights. Over the 100+ years of aviation only 153,000 people have been killed in aviation accidents. There were only 6 fatal accidents in 2017, resulting in 19 fatalities among passengers and crew. This compares with an average of 10.8 fatal accidents and 315 fatalities per year for the 2012–2016 period and with 9 fatal accidents and 202 fatalities in 2016. None of 2017's 6 fatal accidents involved a passenger jet. Of that total, 5 involved turboprop aircraft and 1 involved a cargo jet. The crash of the cargo jet also resulted in 35 fatalities on the ground.

In one of my day job's I work with a number of the 13,000 fellow entrepreneurs in EO (Entrepreneurs Organization) from around the world, leading them in strategy planning and training them to understand how to experience share between each other and to learn from others experiences - the good **and** the bad. This is a proven process I want to bring to in the aviation community.

I became a member of EO in 2000. EO is a global, peer-to-peer network of more than 13,000 influential business owners in 52 countries. Founded in 1987, EO is the catalyst that enables leading entrepreneurs to learn and grow, leading to greater success in business and beyond.

EO employs a unique communication model which provides unparalleled access to the wisdom of your peers during confidential monthly meetings called 'Forum'.

Forum came out of the desire to have a safe environment to share and learn from others' experiences. Extensive research was undertaken to develop the Forum concept. Building from early small group theory, the key objective was to create a safe and supportive environment for members to discuss anything without fear of confidentiality being broken, discuss issues without risk of being judged by others, share, learn and grow with a close group of peers.

EO's Forum offers the opportunity to take risks, opportunities to share information, learn, grow and support each other, experience sharing that spans personal and professional topics, opportunities to share fears and vulnerabilities, the chance to help a peer make a positive change.

When I first started recording my own stories, the first one I wrote down was after an incident here in New Zealand where my brain saw what it wanted to see, which could have ended in disaster. That lesson is detailed in my first book *81 Lessons From The Sky*. I wrote it down to understand the learnings from the incident. And I've shared it so that other pilots won't make the same mistake.

Over a few years, as I read and made notes from aviation stories from around the world, to improve my own aviation knowledge and skills, I realised I had amassed nearly 200 stories, and started trying to work out how to structure the stories to make it easier for other pilots to reference the learnings. I asked a few pilots I knew well whether General Aviation and Air Transport should sit together, i.e. would pilots want to read both? Would they get value from the other stories? Their advice was to split them into two.

In June 2018 I published *81 Lessons From The Sky* - 81 stories from pilots in the General Aviation space and quickly behind it was this book, *101 Lessons From The Sky* - with 101 Air Transport stories.

As a pilot, I now do certain things and operate a certain way so I don't become another statistic. However, in the first few years as a pilot, I did rush and didn't bother trying to understand why certain procedures existed, procedures put in place to ultimately save my life.

These lessons and practices have now become a way of life for me and have spread into other areas in my life - my life practices and life habits.

This book is about lessons from the sky, from real pilots detailing their real experiences and their near misses. Unlike the television shows - *Seconds From Disaster* and *Mayday*, and *Air Crash Investigations*, which document serious accidents or disasters, this book includes stories of incidents and near misses and lessons learnt, from Air Transport pilots, crew and engineers from around the world. Each story giving us an idea of the lessons they learnt.

Enjoy learning and growing.

Fletcher McKenzie

AUSTRALIA - AUS - CASA

Flight Safety Australia:
Civil Aviation Safety Authority

CASA's flagship aviation safety magazine. Topical, technical, but reader-friendly, articles cover all the key aviation safety issues – safety management systems, maintenance, runway safety, human factors, airspace, training, aviation medicine – and more.

Flight Safety Australia, and its predecessor the Aviation Safety Digest, have provided the Australian aviation community with credible and comprehensive aviation safety information since the early 1950s.

From its beginnings as a printed monochrome booklet published only a few times a year, Flight Safety Australia has evolved into an interactive and content-rich publication available across multiple digital platforms.

The website and app keeps readers updated daily. Readers can also experience a stunning interactive digital magazine version for Android and iOS tablets, available by downloading the Flight Safety

Australia app from the relevant app stores. The magazine app is published bi-monthly.

Flight Safety Australia is produced by a small, dynamic team of writers, designers and contributors based out of the Safety Promotion branch of Australia's Civil Aviation Safety Authority. You can access previous issues of Flight Safety Australia online. For editions from 1996 through to April 2014.

Close Calls. The aviation community who have had a close call write to Close Calls about an aviation incident or accident that they have been involved in (as long as it's not the subject of a current official investigation). Written by CASA staff writers unless noted.

With permission we selected a number of stories from in the General Aviation sector.

www.flightsafetyaustralia.com

UNITED KINGDOM - UK - CHIRP

Confidential Human Factors Incident
Report Programme for Aviation

Known by the acronym CHIRP, its aim is to contribute to the
enhancement of flight safety in the UK commercial and general aviation industries, by providing a totally independent confidential
reporting system for all individuals employed in or associated with
the industries.

The Programme is available to engineers and technical staff
involved with the design and manufacturing processes, flight crew
members, cabin crew members, air traffic controllers, licensed engineers and maintenance/engineering personnel and individual aircraft
owners/operators.

CHIRP complements the UK's CAA Mandatory Occurrence
Reporting system and other formal reporting systems operated by
many UK organisations, by providing a means by which individuals
are able to raise safety-related issues of concern without being identified to their peer group, management, or the Regulatory Authority.

CHIRP is a totally independent programme for the collection of confidential safety data, and when appropriate, acting or advising on information gained through confidential reports. Independent advice is provided on aeromedical and Human Factors aspects of reports, involving such topics as errors, fatigue, poor ergonomics, management pressures, deficiencies in communication or team performance. The sensitivity of these topics requires that the anonymity of the reporter must be, and always has been, fully protected.

The CHIRP organisation is comprised of a small team of specialists with professional and technical expertise in commercial aviation and Human Factors. The Programmes are also able to draw on the assistance of a wide range of individual experts and specialist bodies across the spectrum of aviation and maritime sciences in order to promote the resolution of issues raised.

CHIRP® reports are published as a contribution to safety in the aviation industry. FEEDBACK is published quarterly and is circulated in several GA publications throughout the UK.

With permission, we selected a number of stories from the General Aviation FEEDBACK publications.

www.chirp.co.uk

UNITED STATES OF AMERICA - USA - ASRS

Aviation Safety Reporting System

ASRS collects voluntarily submitted aviation safety incident/situation reports from pilots, controllers, and others. It then analyses, and responds to the voluntarily submitted aviation safety incident reports in order to lessen the likelihood of aviation accidents.

ASRS acts on the information these reports contain. It identifies system deficiencies, and issues alerting messages to persons in a position to correct them. It educates through its newsletter CALLBACK, its journal ASRS Directline and through its research studies. Its database is a public repository which serves the FAA and NASA's needs and those of other organisations world-wide which are engaged in research and the promotion of safe flight.

ASRS data are used to identify deficiencies and discrepancies in the National Aviation System (NAS) so that these can be remedied by appropriate authorities. Support policy formulation and planning for, and improvements to, the NAS. Strengthen the foundation of aviation human factors safety research. This is particularly important since it is generally conceded that over two-thirds of all aviation accidents and incidents have their roots in human performance errors.

ASRS's award winning publication CALLBACK is a monthly safety newsletter, which includes de-identified ASRS report excerpts with supporting commentary in a popular "lessons learned" format. In addition, CALLBACK may contain features on ASRS research studies and related aviation safety information. Editorial use and reproduction of CALLBACK articles is encouraged. ASRS appreciates any appropriate attribution of this information. ASRS thanks the aviation community for its interest in and support of CALLBACK.

With permission we selected a number of stories from the CALLBACK publications pertaining to General Aviation.

www.asrs.arc.nasa.gov

CHAPTER 1

AIRWORTHINESS & MAINTENANCE

"In the air transport business more than any other, the human element is everything. That big plane in front of the hangar is only as good as the man who flies it, and he is only as good as the people on the ground who work with him."

W. A. (Pat) Patterson
President
United Airlines

RIGHT SEAL, WRONG PLACE, RETURN TO BASE - CRJ200

CALLBACK

May 2017, Issue 448

[Another] Aircraft Maintenance Technician and I were installing a new carbon seal on the Integrated Drive Generator (IDG) on Engine #1. During that process, we put a seal in the wrong location. We misinterpreted the diagram depicting where the seal went. Throughout this process we had to keep going back to the [Maintenance] Manual to print out sub-tasks using computers that were exceptionally slow, as well as endure many interruptions...which added to our distraction.

After installation, we performed the leak check in accordance with the Maintenance Manual, and there were no leaks, so we did not realize our error at the time. During discussion about the project, supervisors found that we had incorrectly installed the seal. By the time we discovered this fact, it was the following day... The aircraft [had] lost the oil on the left engine IDG, most likely due to our mistake. The aircraft subsequently had to return to base.

It was easy to misinterpret the diagram in the Maintenance Manual. The interruptions due to slow network access to the online Maintenance Manual and [other] interruptions added to the situation.

NOTES:

WHEN YOU'RE OUT OF O2, N2
WON'T DO

CALLBACK

May 2017, Issue 448

[I] received a call... to service oxygen on an [Air Carrier] aircraft. [I] arrived at the scene and opened up the rear tail gate [of the line truck.] I saw one bottle secured to the bed. It was green in color, with no visible warning sign that I can recall. I noticed a steel braided line that was attached to the regulator and wrapped [around] the tail gate, but I did not see the service end. I looked around and found the service kit.... Enclosed was a regulator with a braided line attached. Instead of [switching] regulators, I swapped [the braided] lines and serviced the aircraft with 120 psi of gas.

On my first day back to work [after scheduled days off], I installed what I thought was a missing bottle of nitrogen [in the line truck]. After further inspection, I found that the bottle that was already installed in the truck was nitrogen and not oxygen. I immediately notified my manager of the issue.

I believe that when I looked in the tailgate, I saw a green bottle and didn't see any obvious abnormalities. I assumed the steel braided line was the same type we used in the hangar on the oxygen servicing bottle. The bottle didn't have a...regulator like we had on the high pressure bottle, but [it was] the same color and a similar design.

[I recommend] better placards and warning signs around all gas bottles, more color distinctive regulators used for each [gas] type, and servicing stations at [each] gate.

NOTES:

AN ABUNDANCE OF ASSUMPTIONS - B737

CALLBACK

May 2017, Issue 448

I started my service on a B737 aircraft while another Technician... was to start the fuel nozzle replacements. After I completed my initial service, I noticed that the Number 2 Engine Cowlings were opened up, so I figured that must be the engine getting the fuel nozzles. I found one new nozzle at the In-Station for our plane, so I took it into the Lead's office and told the other Technicians that three were missing, as we were to replace four nozzles altogether. Our Lead was notified and more nozzles were ordered. When they arrived, one Technician took the left side of the engine and another took the right side and began removing the fuel nozzles to replace them. I was the third person, so I was handing tools to them and getting whatever they needed. After the nozzles were replaced, I helped to safety all the bolts that had been removed [and reinstalled]. After Inspectors had looked the engine over for safety and security, I closed Number 2 Engine Cowlings...

The next day I was informed that the nozzles were the wrong

part numbers and that they were supposed to be installed on the Number 1 Engine. I had never looked at any of the paperwork to verify with the other mechanics what part numbers [we were to use] or which engine we were to work on.

NOTES:

OFF WITH THEIR HEADS!

CALLBACK

May 2017, Issue 448

The Maintenance Technician noticed the Nose Gear Steering Cover was loose and seemed to be drooping. He checked the cover and found it to be loose. When attempting to tighten it, he discovered that forward attach bracket screws had been deliberately cutoff and a sealant fabricated screw head was used in its place. At the time the loose steering cover was noticed, the bolts had failed. The event was started by a routine check for a loose steering cover. This is rather common and is simply a hardware tightening process to repair. In this case it turned out to be worse.

The person who installed the steering metering valve missed the step that required the Technician to install the forward attach bracket hardware through the upper steering plate. Apparently after the steering metering valve was installed, the Technician discovered his/her error. Rather than remove the metering valve to correct the error, the Technician opted to cut the screw heads off and use sealant to hold the forward bracket. Note the screw must be installed prior to the steering metering valve installation because there is insufficient clearance with the valve installed.

The aircraft was removed from service. The steering cover was removed and the proper hardware installed. The aircraft was then returned to service.

I suspect that schedule pressure played a role in this event. The Technician, realizing his error, likely feared calling the Inspector to inspect the metering valve reinstallation. The time required to remove and reinstall the valve also would likely need to be explained.

NOTES:

WHO'S ON FIRST?

CALLBACK

May 2017, Issue 448

I was the Lead Mechanic for a propeller build-up during which #2 and #4 Blades were swapped. When the prop was finally put on a plane a month later, the airplane experienced excessive vibration. This is when the prop was inspected and found [to have] blades... installed in the wrong locations.

I think the blades were installed improperly because too many people were involved in the build-up. Blades #1 and #3 were installed first, so I think we just got confused as to which side #2 went on. Inevitably after installing #2 incorrectly, then #4 would also be incorrect. I think we also failed to double-check our work like we did when installing #1 Blade.

NOTES:

ENGINE VIBRATION

CHIRP

Feb 2017, Issue 121

As we were climbing after take-off on our return to base, I had just started preparing to hand out landing cards. I thought that I could feel vibration, so I thought I would quickly go through the cabin and deliver the landing cards but at the same time I would see if I could feel the vibration as I went down the cabin.

Before I could do this, one of my colleagues called on the interphone to report the vibration. As we had both now noticed this I immediately called the flight crew. The reply I got was that the aircraft was "A crock of ****" but not to worry about it! They had felt it too.

During the flight, one of the crew said there was a noise at the back of the cabin like a whining, buzzing bee. I told them to tell the flight crew which they did and was told it was a seal. They said they didn't think it was a seal but felt that they were being patronised and pointed out that if they didn't report these things and if something happened they would have been disciplined if they hadn't reported it. How do things get mended if they aren't reported?

After the flight no mention was made to any of us about our vigilance from the pilots.

Lessons Learned - I would still encourage my crew to be vigilant and report anything they think is unusual, even when at risk of being patronised.

Apparently the company is encouraging a safety culture, but our reporting felt like it wasn't taken seriously or that it was too complicated for us to understand.

CHIRP Comment: Reports from the cabin crew should be received with a positive response. After landing flight crew should take the opportunity to thank the cabin crew, clear up any misunderstandings and indicate whether a tech log entry will be made. Some operators have SOPs to require debriefs following flights in which incidents occur. It is good practice and common courtesy.

NOTES:

FALSIFIED TRAINING RECORDS & WORKING OUTSIDE SCOPE OF APPROVAL OR CAPABILITY

CHIRP

May 2017, Issue 122

A verbal report named a number of individuals and events witnessed, with first-hand knowledge that gave grave concerns regarding individuals working outside of their scope of approval and/or capabilities. A wide ranging discussion took place regarding falsification of experience and training records of Contractors employed through contracting agencies [company names].

CHIRP Comment: The use of contracted engineers and mechanics is increasing, including the use of contractors from abroad. The majority of workers in base maintenance are not required to hold licences but would be supervised by appropriately authorized licence holders. Engineers working as contractors routinely register with several contracting agencies. However, the standard of personal log books is poor and the monitoring and verification of qualifications is difficult to control; a 'passport' system for engineers has been attempted but proved unsuccessful.

Although some employers use the contracting agencies to verify qualifications and conduct induction training, the responsibility lies with the Part 145 rated company, not the contract agency, to ensure the accuracy of training records and competency of any/all persons working under the 145's scope of approval. This should include a review of the contractor's documentation, an interview to determine their previous experience and an assessment of competence if felt necessary. If the contractor has not worked in that organisation previously then training on the company procedures, paperwork and authorisation system should be provided. In the event of doubt about an engineer's licence, employers should contact the license issuing authority. Further advice is available in CAA Information Notice IN-2017/015 entitled Part 145 – Maintenance Staff Employment Status.

NOTES:

PROCEDURAL COMPLACENCY - CRJ-700

CALLBACK

Mar 2017, Issue 446

From the right seat Mechanic's report:

I had performed a Fan Blade Pin change on the Right Engine in accordance with the appropriate work card.... We taxied the aircraft to the testing ramp, and after the required time had elapsed, we began the test by increasing the engine speed to full power. All indications up to this time had been normal... After several seconds at full power, the vibration began to very quickly increase to 1.1... Upon arrival [back] at the hangar, it was discovered that extensive damage had occurred within the engine. I very quickly... discovered that a ratchet I had been using to perform the pin change was missing. I then went to the acting Supervisor's office and reported the damage and my missing tool.

Several factors may have contributed to this incident. It was very early in the morning on my first day back to work after three days off. This is a job I have performed often, and overconfidence or complacency may have figured in.

From the left seat Mechanic's report:

The procedure was not followed.

NOTES:

UNDER PRESSURE - CRJ200

CALLBACK

May 2016, Issue 436

While I worked on a CRJ200 aircraft, two events stemmed from a #1 Main Landing Gear (MLG) tire change that I performed. I received a call from Maintenance Control to inspect damage of a #1 MLG tire. After receiving the limits via fax, I inspected the tire and found it to be beyond limits. Maintenance Control advised a new wheel assembly was going to be sent from another station along with the paperwork. When the wheel arrived, I skimmed through the paperwork and proceeded with the tire change. This is when multiple factors played into the mistakes I made. First: I did not deflate the old tire fully and it was later shipped out by a co-worker. Second: I failed to install a spacer on the new wheel which was not removed from the unserviceable assembly.

I clearly rushed through the Maintenance Manual due to complacency and to get the plane out on time after Maintenance Control stated that the pilots had an hour before they timed out. At the time I thought a tire is a tire, they're all the same. I looked for the key points like torques and safety wiring which ultimately led to my mistakes. It was dark, which added to my missing the spacer and I did not have the proper tool on hand to deflate the tire, which led me to only partially deflating it. I know what I did was wrong and I definitely learned from it. I will never again jeopardize my licenses and career like this.

NOTES:

CHAPTER 2

COMPLACENCY & FATIGUE

"There are no new types of air crashes — only people with short memories. Every accident has its own forerunners, and every one happens either because somebody did not know where to draw the vital dividing line between the unforeseen and the unforeseeable or because well-meaning people deemed the risk acceptable."

Stephen Barlay

The Final Call: Why Airline Disasters Continue to Happen

March 1990

FUNCTIONAL COMPLACENCY - B767-300

CALLBACK

Mar 2017, Issue 446

After becoming airborne on our initial takeoff, the Captain called, "Gear up." Inexplicably, I raised the flap handle instead of the gear handle. Over the next several seconds, the flaps retracted while I confirmed lateral navigation (LNAV) at 400 feet AGL, selected vertical navigation (VNAV) at 1,000 feet AGL, and responded to Tower's call to change to Departure Control. During this time, the flaps were retracting, and the minimum airspeed indicator "hook" increased until the stick shaker activated. When this happened, I looked at the flap indicator, realized my error, and extended the flaps to takeoff position (Flaps 5). Simultaneously, the Captain reduced the climb angle, I raised the gear handle, the aircraft accelerated, and the stick shaker stopped. The rest of the departure was normal.

I screwed up... No excuses. I have no idea why I reached for the flaps instead of the gear. I have successfully raised the gear—without error—for decades and buckets of hours. Slow down. Don't rush. Fight complacency. Don't think it can't happen to you!

NOTES:

COMBATING COMPLACENCY

CALLBACK

Mar 2017, Issue 446

This report is to highlight my concern about personnel who are not active working crew members on a flight (jump-seaters), but take it upon themselves to arm and disarm aircraft doors. I have personally had this situation happen, and I have witnessed it happening to fellow working crew members.

My intent... is to bring to the attention of the company... an action that should be discouraged and discontinued due to its ability to impact the safety and security of an armed aircraft door... I think a note or bulletin needs to be sent out to each and every flight attendant explaining proper procedures so that complacency does not breed an opportunity for a fatal outcome.

NOTES:

NOT A GOOD FRIDAY - B99

CALLBACK

Jan 2016, Issue 432

Enroute ... I started to perform my required "Weekly Checks" Checklist, going through item by item. The checklist calls for the weekly fire-test; the first item is to pull both fire handles. As I pulled them I noticed a sudden loss of performance on both engines. My gauges indicated that both of them flamed out. I pushed the handles back and started to troubleshoot. I determined that my right engine was still operational. Meanwhile, the aircraft was losing altitude but it was under control. I advised ATC about my situation and they told me there was an airport ten miles away along my route.... Being a new pilot on this airplane, under these circumstances I decided the best course of action was to secure the inoperative engine and land as soon as possible. Having my right engine operational, I was able to stabilize the airplane and started my VFR descent. I completed my Emergency Checklist and then performed a safe single engine landing.

I am a new pilot on this airplane, having just completed my upgrade training one week ago. During the flight training, this part of the checklist was never mentioned and the checklist was not available in the training aircraft. On the checklist, the fire test appears to be among the inflight test items. This situation was the result of me following the checklist that I believed I was supposed to perform. Had I received the proper training, I am sure this situation could have been avoided.

NOTES:

CLIMB TO INCREASE AIRSPEED - ERJ-145

CALLBACK

Jan 2016, Issue 432

On the takeoff roll, after calling out, "Thrust set," I scanned the EICAS engine indications, and then I fixated on the altimeter, confusing it with the airspeed indicator. When the numbers on the altimeter dial did not increase during the takeoff roll, I mistakenly believed it was a stuck airspeed indication and called for an aborted takeoff. The Captain aborted the takeoff and we taxied to a location where we could talk to maintenance. As I was explaining to the Captain what I had seen, I realized my mistake. I had confused the Altimeter indication with the Airspeed. There were no problems with the aircraft and we completed the flight safely.

NOTES:

BAD VIBRATIONS - A320

CALLBACK

Jan 2016, Issue 432

We were focused on avoiding thunderstorms in the departure corridor. Immediately after takeoff we requested a right turn from Departure. We also remained vigilant of the [reported traffic]. There was now another concentrated area of weather directly ahead. I was trying to break into the congested Departure frequency for a turn on course, which would provide adequate weather clearance. This took a couple minutes and dominated our attention.

I noticed a slight airframe rumbling, but thought it might be the landing lights which were still extended. Once we were given the turn on course and accelerated to 250 knots, we both started to focus on the increasing noise and vibration. I raised the landing lights with very little improvement. We completely concentrated on things that might be wrong with the airplane and searched through numerous system ECAM pages for answers. Everything appeared normal and all symbols were green (including the large green landing gear DOWN and LOCKED symbols which were as we always see them... on the ground. But the gear doors I concentrated on were in fact UP and green), so we started hypothesizing about abnormal things that might be wrong with the jet. Things like a missing engine cowl, flap track fairings, gear doors open, flight controls out of position. We continued north as we attempted troubleshooting and began to think about diverting. We asked the Lead Flight Attendant to take a look at the wings, etc. and report back any anomalies. He found nothing unusual. I asked the First Officer to keep the speed back at 210 knots and to level off at 15,000 feet to remain in a safe speed and altitude range in case something was extended and to protect the airframe. I attempted a radio patch through Dispatch to include Maintenance. The reception was poor and we never spoke with Maintenance. We decided to continue communications through ACARS.

Enough troubleshooting time had passed that I decided we needed to get the plane on the ground safely. I instructed the First Officer to coordinate landing at the divert airport while I briefed the Lead Flight Attendant and then performed the Airframe Vibration Checklist... As the First Officer flew the visual approach he called for "Gear Down, Landing Checklist." It then became immediately clear that our "problem" was that the landing gear had never been retracted. We continued to a landing without incident since there was not enough time to verify adequate fuel to continue to [our destination].

I attribute this error to saturation with weather and traffic avoidance on departure followed by a lack of performing normal climb out procedures for the same reason.... When we were handed off to Departure we focused intently on clearing traffic and weather on a very congested frequency. Obviously, I did not raise the gear and after raising the flaps we had already completed our 90-degree right turn and were headed toward the thunderstorm area directly ahead. My attention was primarily on trying to break into the busy Departure Control frequency for an immediate clearance north away from the weather. This dominated our attention and I believe I never accomplished the After Takeoff Checklist since it's simply so out of sequence climbing out of approximately five or six thousand feet.

Between us, [the First Officer and I] have around 30,000 flight hours, and about eight years' experience each in the Airbus. I believe this is an important contributing factor since I have never experienced even a delayed gear retraction on takeoff. It's such an unusual thing that we simply didn't consider it. As we scrolled through ECAM system pages and other troubleshooting attempts/hypotheses, we never considered such a simple error. Our experience level led us directly to troubleshooting a problem rather than looking for the obvious solution. It's the most embarrassing event of my flying career.

This flight encountered a confluence of operational challenges as well as human factors issues which resulted in a sub-par performance. It's not like we lacked understanding of landing gear panel or ECAM symbols. I simply allowed my focus on weather and aircraft avoidance to lead to my neglect of basics. I failed to raise the landing gear and perform the After Takeoff Checklist properly since we were so far past the normal flight sequence to accomplish it while concentrating on immediate safety of flight procedures.... I am glad the company allowed us to continue the flight since I personally wanted to get back in the saddle and put this behind us.

NOTES:

PRESSURE TO FLY WHEN NOT FIT

CHIRP

May 2017, Issue 122

I had a call yesterday from a manager to be informed that my absence record had resulted in me being placed in Company's absence management programme. For this to happen, I had 3 separate absences due to being medically unfit. I was told that I am not allowed to call sick for another 12 months or I will be put into a more serious level of the programme. I asked how I could be expected to defy the laws of nature and stop being human and know that I was not going to be ill for 12 months. The answer was that I had to achieve this.

This puts huge pressure on me. Despite the fact that I will protect my licence and not come to work sick, I have to live with this stress over me for 12 months. If I am sick, who knows what happens next (the manager refused to tell me). I am lucky that my pension is the old type which will not be affected if I am put into the next phase of the process, but for newer guys, there are huge financial implications of being sick. It is [wrong] of [the Company] to put this pressure on their pilots to report for work unfit and I would like to know why the CAA are letting them get away with it!?!

CHIRP Comment: It is understandable that operators wish to minimise absences from work but the obligations of licence holders to fly only when fully fit should be factored into absence management programmes. Multiple absences may require occupational health assessment to determine the cause(s) but flight crew should not be made to feel under pressure to fly when not fit. The reporter is correct; no matter what the potential implications, pilots should only fly when they are fit to do so. If unfit to work through illness pilots should seek aeromedical advice from their AME thus ensuring the episode of illness is documented.

NOTES:

FATIGUE

CHIRP

Feb 2017, Issue 121

I was rostered for a series of early morning starts with report times varying from 0505 to 0555 LT. I live one hour from the crew car park and it generally takes 20 minutes to park and get the bus to the crew reporting point. With the best will in the world and the most efficient preparation, I still need to set the alarm to 03:30 to make the earliest report.

I did my best during this series of duties to manage rest, taking some catch up naps during the afternoon after getting home and going to bed at a reasonably early time. By the evening before the last duty I was so tired that I went to bed and fell asleep at 8pm, waking at 0400 having had a full 8 hours sleep. For the first time in this series of duties I felt well rested; but the events of the day were to show that this was merely an illusion.

I made series of small mistakes, starting with such things as reading the wrong line on the performance figures, then omitting to delete a redundant stop altitude from the FMC; things got worse as after takeoff during flap retraction I was first asked, as is normal, to select flap 1 and then later flap Up. When I came to make the selection to Up, I discovered that I had already selected flaps Up when asked for Flap 1, despite the fact that there is a mechanical gate at the Flap 1 position designed to prevent exactly this happening. Fortunately the aircraft was light and accelerating so fast that the lift margin was never compromised. I had no recollection of doing that at all. Further minor errors occurred throughout the flight (no lights on as we descended) and I arrived back at base feeling very unprofessional and embarrassed.

The lesson here is that your level of fatigue is not necessarily a function of how fatigued you feel! I have noticed this effect before when awaking for an early and feeling great, but not actually performing so great. Oddly when I feel very tired I think my brain subconsciously makes sure I try harder!

It was for this reason I stopped using one of those clever smartphone apps (sleep cycle) which monitors your sleeping cycles and only wakes you at the peak of a cycle; correctly claiming that you feel better having woken at a state of light sleep. You might well feel better, but that doesn't guarantee you will perform better.

In my opinion it seems that sometimes fatigue can be insidious - rather like hypoxia. You think it's going well, but it isn't!

I'd be interested if there is any research along these lines to confirm this idea?

CHIRP Comment: We are pleased to be able to print this honest report about the insidious nature of fatigue. EASA FTLs require operators to conduct fatigue management training but the recognition of fatigue is not specifically included:

ORO.FTL.250 Fatigue Management Training

(a) 'insert airline name' shall provide initial and recurrent fatigue management training to crew members, personnel responsible for preparation and maintenance of crew rosters and management personnel concerned.

(b) This training shall follow a training programme established by 'insert airline name' and described in the operations manual. The training syllabus shall cover the possible causes and effects of fatigue and fatigue countermeasure.

However, AMC1 ORO.FTL.250 states the FRM training syllabus should contain the following:

(b) the basics of fatigue including sleep fundamentals and the effects of disturbing the circadian rhythms" and "the effect of fatigue on performance.

Some operators do include training about recognising fatigue in oneself and others but the reporter has correctly highlighted the practical difficulty of reliably recognising fatigue in oneself on a day-to-day basis. There is research about fatigue that includes observations about its insidious nature. "The Cumulative Cost of Additional Wakefulness: Dose-Response Effects on Neurobehavioral Functions and Sleep Physiology from Chronic Sleep Restriction and Total Sleep Deprivation" (Van Dongen et al; "Sleep2 Vol 26 No 2 2003.) examined the effect of sleep deprivation on cognitive function. Its conclusions include, "... it appears that even relatively moderate sleep restriction can seriously impair waking neurobehavioral functions in healthy adults. Sleepiness ratings suggest that subjects were largely unaware of these increasing cognitive deficits.." This conclusion appears to provide scientific evidence to support the reporter's contention that the effects of fatigue are insidious.

NOTES:

REPORTING FATIGUE TO THE COMPANY

CHIRP

May 2017, Issue 122

I offloaded myself in the middle of a long sequence of Flight Duty Periods where every day involved multiple sectors. After checking out, I filled in the fatigue report form. I then had to call crewing, who wanted me to report back the next morning to position to [ ] to carry on with my roster (I had been due to operate there the evening before). Crewing also wanted me to call them the next morning to let them know whether or not I was still fatigued.

I did call crewing the next morning (having set my alarm to ensure I was awake in time call them with enough notice to call a standby to cover my duty) to let them know I was still exhausted. So what do our good friends in crewing do on my roster? They put me down as SICK.

The following Sunday morning, when I was well rested, I reported to continue my roster. Before flying I [had an interview to determine the circumstances and background to my reporting fatigue]. May I say that the interview did not feel like a duty of care interview, but more an interrogation into my lifestyle?

A few days later I received an email asking me to fill in a Self-Certification form for my recent sickness. [The explanation was that my absence had been recorded] as sickness as my roster met the legal requirements when it was put through [a proprietary fatigue management application].

So, not only are the company relying on computer software to decide whether or not a flight crew member is fatigued, they have also made the whole process of reporting fatigue very long-winded. Having spoken to a number of flight crew within the company, I discover that - for the sake of simplicity - flight crew are actually reporting sick rather than going through the whole fatigue reporting process.

CHIRP Comment: Reporting sick, rather than fatigued, for convenience cannot be condoned. It is reasonable for operators to investigate the factors contributing to fatigue in order to identify the elements that are their responsibility to manage. Unfortunately, susceptibility to fatigue is dependent on individual personal characteristics and circumstances and therefore a great deal of information is required. It might be a time consuming process but it is necessary to gather the information either by a filling in a long fatigue reporting form or subsequently by interview.

Fatigue modelling software is becoming increasingly sophisticated but should not be used as a determinant of whether a particular individual was fatigued. There needs to be a clear policy on reporting fatigue, including how and who classifies it and clear training on the use of models to support fatigue assessment. It is reasonable that the impact of the individual circumstances is considered as well but if a crew member says they were too fatigued to operate then they were and the information needs to be recorded.

NOTES:

SLEEP LESS IN SEATTLE - B737

CALLBACK

July 2016, Issue 438

After being assigned FL390 and a subsequent frequency change, we discovered during the climb that we had leveled at FL380 for approximately 10 minutes. I was the Pilot Flying, but when we changed Center frequencies, I took the call. When I checked in, I stated our altitude (FL380) and, as is my habit pattern, looked at the Mode Control Panel (MCP) altitude window. It read 39,000 and was different from our current altitude, so I checked in by saying, "Seattle, (call sign) FL380, climbing FL390." I had not noticed that we had been level at FL380 for approximately 10 minutes. I simply assumed we were still slowly climbing to our cruise altitude.... I looked at the MCP altitude window again. It read 39,000. I told Seattle it looked like we were climbing to FL390 but we were level at FL380. Seattle said to climb to FL390. I affirmed that clearance. The Captain also confirmed the clearance over the radio and we climbed to FL390 without incident.

In retrospect, I realize that I had probably entered FL380 into the FMC on the ground before we had received our new paperwork....

This was the last leg of an extremely taxing four-day trip that would have been illegal prior to FAR 117. I was more tired than I realized.... I cannot over-emphasize the importance of fatigue in situations like this. I didn't realize how tired I was.

First Impressions Don't Always Last

NOTES:

A REJECTED TAKEOFF

CALLBACK

July 2016, Issue 438

I was the First Officer and Pilot Flying for this [international] night flight. It was the seventh of eight duty periods and my second of two opportunities in the right seat on this trip. Our preflight preparation was completed for an on time pushback. The weather was VFR, we were heavy at 618,000 pounds, and our first opportunity on the runway resulted in a rejected takeoff.

With the Non Flying Pilot callout of "80 knots," I recall a quick scan of the Primary Flight Display (PFD), but did not linger to verify 80 [knots] and the green trend line on the PFD speed tape. I believe I instinctively made the inappropriate callout "checked," but was troubled enough to make at least two quick scans back to the PFD. Regrettably, both times when I glanced down, I saw the right side altitude tape instead of the left side speed tape, and what [registered incorrectly as airspeed] in my mind both times was 40, which was, in reality, the takeoff zone elevation.

Company training kicked in for a perceived malfunction, but I struggled to call it out clearly and precisely. Nevertheless, I commu-

nicated the threat and we accomplished the rejected takeoff procedure. When I saw the functioning and decreasing speed tape, my
error became clear. There was, in fact, no frozen 40 [knot airspeed]
indication. With a safe stop assured...I briefed the Captain on
my error.

I have beaten myself up over it, but still can't pinpoint the root
cause. [Was it] fatigue on a long trip or less than usual currency in the
seat for me? [Was it] a distraction with the centerline lighting, or was
the PFD lighting too low? Nevertheless, vigilance and the commit-
ment to speak up are traits that we have emphasized and I took them
to heart.

NOTES:

TARGET FIXATION

CALLBACK

July 2016, Issue 438

From the Captain's Report

We were maintaining 6,000 feet to join the ILS for Runway 11L. Four miles prior to the Initial Approach Fix I selected Heading Mode and inadvertently hit the transfer button causing the ILS frequency to disappear in the Communications 1 standby box. I was distracted by this and tried to fix it. I was fixated on my [ILS] frequency and did not recognize that the autopilot had disconnected. The Pilot Not Flying asked what was wrong. I [corrected] the frequency error and looked up to see that we were low for the approach and then the Ground Proximity Warning System (GPWS) "Too Low Terrain" alert went off. I applied max thrust and started to climb. ATC also said that they were getting a Low Altitude Alert and suggested the 6,000 foot minimum vectoring altitude in that sector. We climbed back through 6,000 feet, leveled off, intercepted the ILS to Runway 11L, and continued the approach.

    The day was long with weather in the entire southwest. We flew five legs and were delayed...every leg. An ILS was hampered by fatigue and [selecting] the wrong button on the Communications 1 standby box, followed by fixation on that problem. Fatigue being the cause, a solution is to avoid and recognize it before it hampers safety.

From the First Officer's Report

The uncommon weather conditions, turbulence throughout every flight, and long delays most likely contributed to our being fatigued.... It appears that fatigue and fixation on a communication [switching] problem were the causes.

NOTES:

DON'T PUT OFF UNTIL TOMORROW WHAT YOU CAN DO TODAY

CALLBACK

July 2016, Issue 438

I was instructed to meet the aircraft to conduct routine maintenance that consisted of an oil change and an inspection required by an Airworthiness Directive (AD). The aircraft arrived at dusk and I proceeded to drain the oil, remove and replace the oil filter, add new oil, and complete the inspection. Because it was not common company practice to cut open and inspect every oil filter removed from an aircraft, I set the old oil filter aside to drain and did nothing more with it. I had been on duty for twelve hours and was eager to finish the maintenance and go home.

The aircraft departed early the next morning. That afternoon the aircraft experienced a catastrophic engine failure and made a forced landing.

Some weeks later another maintenance technician located and cut open the oil filter that I had removed. Upon inspection, the filter was glittering with ferrous and non-ferrous metal, an obvious indication that the engine was not airworthy and required immediate attention. Had I cut open and inspected the filter the evening it was removed, I would never have signed off the aircraft as airworthy and the incident would have been avoided.

I believe several factors contributed to this occurrence.... A long duty day and consequent fatigue likely inhibited my better judgment to cut and inspect the oil filter.

NOTES:

DOUBLE CHECKING THE CHECK VALVE

CALLBACK

July 2016, Issue 438

I was tasked with the functional check of the Number 1 engine low stage bleed check valve. While reinstalling the valve, I accidentally installed it backwards. After it was put back together we [ran] the engine. On the first engine run we had a Bleed-1 Fail message. We reset everything and ran the engine again at power with the APU bleed off. This time no message came into view. We ran the engine a few more times...and didn't receive any abnormal indications.

The next morning the aircraft returned to the gate with a write-up...the number one engine [had] shut down on takeoff roll at thirty percent power. At Maintenance Control's direction, we returned to the hangar to verify the check valve installation and found that it had been improperly installed.

At the time of re-install I had been up for approximately 18 hours. This is a job I have done before and I am familiar with it. I was tired and installed it incorrectly. I was fatigued and not aware...that I had installed it backwards.

NOTES:

INCREASED RISK LEVELS

CHIRP

January 2018, Issue 125

I'm sitting in [ ] filling out another ASR and have realised, after reading back my description of events, that an ASR doesn't begin to highlight my concern with the current level of risk we are exposing ourselves to.

There is currently a disagreement between our union and the Company. One element of it is that flight crew don't, as a matter of course, acknowledge any roster changes or delays communicated outside contractually obligated contact periods.

For us, flying the Freighter, this no contact has a huge impact on our roster stability. The roster is very fluid, to say the least, and what has become normalised deviancy is to turn up to work at home-base to pick up a long delay. Often this can result in running out of flight duty times at sign-on, or usually just to delay a flight into or further into our WOCL, as most flights are back-of-the-body-clock anyway. We'll leave knock-on effects and parking jets to another day.

So, the plan: unusually, an early evening sign on, one quick sector, all done and in the hotel by 0200 body clock.

Get to work in time for a leisurely coffee and flight prep to find a 3:30 hr delay due to landing slots at either my destination, or the next. The new take-off time is now at scheduled landing time. The whole plan for home/work/rest is now invalid and I haven't signed on yet. The delay pushes the flight into WOCL; we won't now get to the hotel much before 05:00L and the approach will be at 04:00L (and body-clock). Two-man crew, we both had a relatively early start to try to keep some semblance of home/work balance, so a long day. I ask for a hotel room to rest, and mitigate some fatigue, but crewing refuse the request as the delay was deemed too short to qualify i.a.w company procedures.

We sit around dispatch for 3 1/2 hours, decide we feel good enough for the duty, get to the aircraft where we find further delays due to flow control (another 35 mins as it turns out, but originally ATC were talking about another 2-3 hours). OK, we are here, both feeling awake, full of caffeine, FTLs still OK, short flight, happy to continue.

The flight is '[ ] standard', poor comms, wrong levels, more fuel burn, summer weather avoids en route and unforecast arrival weather, and, to top it off, an appalling, high workload feed-in to the ILS. All-in-all another day in the office.

I am a great fan of the old Swiss-Cheese accident model and there are a whole series of holes from this one example, all lining up, and more importantly, becoming the accepted norm. We, as individuals are implementing solutions to mitigate the elevated levels of risk in the operations but we need fundamental changes at the top before a major incident occurs. 'We could see it happening, it was only a matter of time' is never an acceptable posture and I feel we have been frogs in warming water for so long, the water is beginning to boil. I have heard there are improvements in the pipeline, but change is notoriously slow in this company. We are the last line of defence, we are at that last line, there are holes in that last line.....

CHIRP Comment: The Operator confirmed that it was aware of the fatigue issue and had several initiatives to address it, including a new crew management programme, new rostering software and a fully integrated FRMS. The operator agreed with the reporter's analysis that the disagreement between itself and the Union resulted in crew members not checking changes to flight schedules, delays and duty times before coming to work and, as such, crews were not aware if there was a significant change to a duty. This resulted in unnecessary early reports when crew members could be at home resting rather than waiting at an airport or in dispatch. This was not the only reason for roster disruption but contributed significantly. From the CHIRP perspective it is clear that there are safety implications associated with this dispute. All involved are urged to do their utmost to resolve it urgently.

NOTES:

CHAPTER 3

HUMAN FACTORS & DECISION MAKING

"We are unable, we may end up in the Hudson."
Chesley B. 'Sully' Sullenberger
Captain of US Airways flight 1549

WHEN IS AN ENGINE FAILURE NOT AN ENGINE FAILURE?

CHIRP

Nov 2016, Issue 120

My report is seeking Regulator clarification of whether in flight, an engine that is not capable of full thrust, can be taken to be an engine that has NOT failed.

It has been brought to my attention by a member of our training department, that the QRH for our twin engine aircraft, only demands we land at the nearest suitable airport in the event of a total engine failure, that is an engine that is not producing any thrust at all. He stated clearly and repeatedly, that an engine that is not producing sufficient thrust for safe flight on that one engine alone, can be used to enable continued flight to destination. So, if you have an uncontrolled rollback that no longer responds to thrust lever inputs, the QRH for a surging or stalled engine does not demand a landing at the nearest suitable airfield, even when the engine is at idle and does not respond to any thrust lever input at all. The same would be true for any running engine that is not able to produce full thrust for whatever reason. The instructor was quite adamant about this, and responded vigorously to my argument that this was not a correct interpretation of our procedures. He is right that such a rollback would require use of a checklist that does not require a landing as soon as possible, but airmanship demands that an aircraft that now has only one fully serviceable engine between it and an accident, is one that should be landed as soon as practicable.

Is it possible that the instructor is wrong? To me it sounded awfully like management hogwash, and that a crew that decided to continue normal flight to destination, passing any number of 'suitable airfields' en route with only one fully serviceable engine, would immediately be invited for tea, no biscuits, with the regulator to explain himself. However, this argument, that the QRH seems to allow such an operation needs clarification, because the level of pressure now being exerted on crews to toe the company line is so strong as to influence all but the bravest of the brave. I struggle to see how this can be a correct interpretation. Your input will be appreciated.

Lessons Learned:

That it is possible that an airman's understanding of airmanship is no longer enough. We may now need a legal definition of airmanship, based on loopholes in the company manuals which have therefore been 'authorised' by the regulator. The unwritten will become the hole through which we are legally encouraged to jump, no matter how unsafe. The third crew member may yet reappear, but this time in the form of a legal advisor, rather like the old dog and a pilot in the cockpit joke. His role will be to monitor our decisions and tell us when we have no legal mandate to take action X, where less safe but legal action Y is available, and of course action Y will always be to the company's operational and financial advantage.

CHIRP Comment: It is both normal and correct that there should be a safety investigation following a serious incident in order to determine whether there are lessons to be learned. However, flight crew should not be concerned about their vulnerability to disciplinary or legal action provided their decisions are made in a professional manner using all of the information available to them. If the checklist does not mandate a diversion, it is very much a decision for the Captain on the day, taking in to account the nature of the engine problem. If there is insufficient information to diagnose the nature of an engine problem in a twin engine aircraft, a diversion would be appropriate. Similarly, if an engine is not doing what it should or is unable to keep the aircraft airborne on its own and a single-engine approach is appropriate, the aircraft should be diverted. The decision making skill of a Captain could be questioned if he/she continued the flight beyond an airfield at which a safe landing could be made, if an engine was malfunctioning but still running.

NOTES:

LOW FUEL PRESS

CALLBACK

April 2017, Issue 447

Early during the takeoff roll, the pilot noted a right hand LOW FUEL PRESS annunciator and associated Master Warning... All [other] aircraft instruments and indications remained normal.

The pilot rejected the takeoff, as briefed, for a Master Warning prior to V1 speed. The pilot assumed a false annunciator warning because the LOW FUEL PRESS annunciator extinguished after power was reduced...and all other remaining instruments and annunciators were indicating normal. The pilot decided to attempt a normal takeoff after taxiing back to [the] runway and receiving takeoff clearance. All operations during the second takeoff were entirely normal and routine, with no abnormal annunciations or events. The flight continued through termination under normal operating circumstances.

NOTES:

APPROACHING MINIMUMS

CALLBACK

April 2017, Issue 447

The marine fog bank had just come in. As we were intercepting the course for the RNAV Y RWY 27 approach, several planes ahead of us all went around. Tower gave us a short delay vector off the course and re-cleared us on the LOC RWY 27 approach. We did a very quick and dirty brief, noting...managed/selected [speeds] and [a potential] missed approach. I loaded the FMC while the Captain flew. I felt we were being rushed with the last minute approach change, and...it was only my third flight [in the last month]. I was slower than normal and a bit rusty as well. I didn't notice that the Derived Decision Altitude (DDA) I set was above the 500 feet AGL call. As we neared the minimums, I was looking to make the 500 feet call and completely missed the 100 feet above "Approaching Minimums" call and subsequently was late with the "Minimums" call also. The Captain called "Minimums" for me followed by his "Going Around" call. He pushed the thrust levers up to the go around detent, called "Flaps 3," and began to pitch up. I was still a second or two behind him thinking about the minimums call I just missed and didn't immediately retract the flaps. Before I could set the flaps to three, the Captain said that the runway was in sight.

The First Officer's Action

We had hit a hole in the clouds, and the runway was there. We were still configured and in position to make a safe landing.

The Captain's Action

A second or two after bringing up the power, we were in the clear with the runway in sight. Since the flaps and gear had not been moved yet, I chose to pitch over gently and continued visually to land in the touchdown zone with a normal rate of descent and normal landing.

NOTES:

STORM OVER THE AIRPORT

CALLBACK

April 2017, Issue 447

We departed with good weather forecast for Salt Lake City with no alternate needed. We were planned with 600 pounds of taxi fuel and 1,471 pounds of contingency fuel. The flight was uneventful until we began the descent to SLC. We were being vectored north around the airport to get around a storm that was over the airport. As we broke out north of the airport, I looked down and saw it raining on the east side with more storms east of the airport. We were on downwind vectors for [runway] 16L and had just been cleared for the approach when ATC said that aircraft were reporting a loss of 20 knots indicated airspeed (KIAS) on final and were going around. I told the FO to tell them we will be discontinuing the approach and would like to hold for a bit. We were still doing alright on fuel then and had 3,800 pounds on board. I figured we had 10 to 15 minutes before we had to do an approach to SLC or divert.... I was focused on whether or not we could hold long enough to get into SLC. ATC said that the storm was passing at SLC, and the winds were 16 knots and steady with no Low Level Windshear alerts. They asked if we would like to do an approach. We decided that we would try a single approach, and if we went missed, [then we would] go to ZZZ. We setup for the approach, intercepted final, and started configuring flaps. ATC advised heavy precipitation between us and the runway.

We were on the glideslope at 190 KIAS with flaps 2 passing through 7,500 feet MSL when it seems we might have encountered a microburst.... Within 5 seconds our indicated airspeed rapidly increased to 234 KIAS.

I would have normally broken off the approach immediately, but we were high enough off the ground that I could get stable by 1,000 feet AGL, and I also expected the [air]speed increase to immediately subside. We were both caught completely off guard when the airspeed didn't go back to normal, but actually kept increasing. At that point, I told ATC that we were going missed and going to ZZZ.... Even though there was a flap overspeed, I elected to retract the flaps due to our fuel status and not knowing if there would be a delay getting into ZZZ with other aircraft being diverted there. I felt it would be less risky to retract the flaps than to continue flying with the flaps at 2 and burn extra fuel. We landed at ZZZ uneventfully, and I left the flaps in the landing configuration until Maintenance could look at them.

NOTES:

THE GO-AROUND - B737

CALLBACK

April 2017, Issue 447, First Officer's Report

While on approach, we started out a little high due to thunderstorms that were on our arrival. The deviation was going to get us on the ground with about 6,400 pounds of fuel. Just north of the airport, we were turned onto a downwind and cleared to 4,000 feet MSL, and after that to 3,000 feet. Once we got close to leveling off at 3,000 feet, we were given a base turn...and cleared down to 2,600 feet. At that time we reported the airport in sight, and I noticed that we were still around 240 KIAS. I queried the Captain if he still wanted to go that fast. He said he had not realized we were still going that fast and started slowing. He dropped the gear and started slowing while also following the glide slope. I made the 1,000 foot call, but we both realized we only had flaps 15 selected up until that point. We missed that gate, but it looked like the aircraft was slowing enough to make the 500 foot gate. As we tried to get the aircraft slowed, I think we may have had only flaps 25 at the 500 foot gate.

I should have made the go-around call per Standard Operating Procedure (SOP). However, neither of us announced the go-around, and we continued to land.... Luckily, we landed uneventfully. As we taxied clear of the runway, we both agreed that we should have gone around and, after the fact, realized our non-compliance. I realized that I should have used my training and my assertiveness to announce the go-around per SOP. I still regret not speaking up as I should have.

NOTES:

A BELLY LANDING - LR-24

CALLBACK

Oct 2016, Issue 441, Pilot's Report

We were departing a small...airport when a light twin landed [with a] gear malfunction [that] resulted in a belly landing. [That] aircraft came to rest in a position leaving approximately 4,000 feet of runway unobstructed.

At [that] time, we had only started the number 2 engine and were sitting on the FBO ramp, having not moved from our initial parked position.... I began to deplane so I could offer assistance to the disabled aircraft... The Captain stopped me and told me to sit down... I objected, but [he] told me that he was keeping our schedule. He proceeded to taxi, and I had to stop him from blocking the path for an emergency vehicle. After the fire truck passed, several airport officials, two of whom were in uniform, crossed their arms over their heads and attempted to stop [our] taxi. I brought this to the Captain's attention... but he proceeded to start the number 1 engine on the taxi roll, disregarding any checklist. Multiple aircraft on the approach to the airport reported, via UNICOM, that they were diverting because of the fouled runway.

As the Captain entered the runway, I brought it to his attention that we needed 3,600 feet of runway according to the performance data for the airplane to safely take off. I questioned the wisdom of taking off on approximately 4,000 feet of runway with a disabled aircraft with passengers and emergency crews still in close proximity. The Captain turned around with about 25 [feet of] clearance to the fire truck, and, over my objection, he initiated a takeoff.

NOTES:

A FUEL IMBALANCE - B767

CALLBACK

Oct 2016, Issue 441, Captain's Report

[Enroute to our destination], the crew noticed a fuel imbalance situation developing between the left and right main tanks with approximately 2,700 pounds remaining in the center tank. The left main fuel tank had approximately 40,000 pounds and the right had approximately 38,000 pounds with the "FUEL CONFIG" light illuminated. The crew balanced the fuel between tanks, [but also] noticed that the fuel quantity in the center tank was increasing slightly. The QRH was consulted. Nothing there seemed to apply to this situation. We relayed all the information up to that point to the Maintenance Representative.... The rate of transfer from the right main tank to the center was approximately 3,100 pounds per hour. At that point we were informed by the Maintenance Representative that once the main tanks reached the halfway point in their burn (about 20,000 pounds per tank), the fuel transfer from the right tank to the center would cease.

I elected to continue the flight expecting to land [at our planned destination] with approximately 18,000 pounds in the center and approximately 8,000 pounds in each main tank. We put together a plan to divert to several locations as the situation developed. We then spent time figuring out various scenarios to determine the options for safety, weather, maintenance, passenger servicing, etc. We climbed to FL380 as soon as ATC allowed it, [achieving] slightly better range and enroute weather avoidance. As we approached [one of the diversion locations], it became clear that [we] would not reach [our original destination] safely. We declared an emergency and elected to divert to [this newly chosen location]. At that point the fuel tanks had about 16,000 pounds in each main tank and approximately 18,000 to 19,000 pounds in the center. By the time we reached [this diversion airport], the main tanks were down to approximately 5,500 pounds, [with] the center at 35,000 pounds and climbing. We were given direct [to a fix] for the ILS. Not feeling comfortable with the distance from the end of the runway, we called, "Field in sight," and headed directly toward the end of the runway.... I felt [that] the [threat] of losing one or both engines was a real possibility. I was determined to get to a 3-mile final with at least 2,000 feet to 2,500 feet of altitude in case of a dual engine failure. Once we were close enough to the field we flew through final to gain spacing, and...were in the slot by 500 feet. [We] landed without incident [with] approximately 2,500 pounds in the left and 2,000 pounds in the right tank as we crossed the threshold.

NOTES:

THRUST LEVER JAMMED - CRJ-200

CALLBACK

Oct 2016, Issue 441, Captain's Report

After leveling off at FL310, the number 1 engine power could not be reduced. The thrust lever was completely unresponsive. After trying to troubleshoot the problem, we both looked in the QRH and decided that the only checklist for our situation was, "Thrust Lever Jammed."... We called Maintenance on the radio to see if they might have a suggestion, [but they had no advice for our predicament].

We told the Flight Attendant we were going to shut down the engine and that it would be a normal landing. We checked the weather [at] nearby alternates to see if conditions were any better than [they were at our] destination, but they were worse. We declared an emergency, got vectors to run the checklists, made the announcement to the passengers, and landed with no further problems.... The flight crew did exactly as we were trained, and it resulted in a successful conclusion. At no time were we in any doubt about what we were doing and what the results would be.

NOTES:

DISCHARGING AMMETER - C182

CALLBACK

Feb 2016, Issue 433, Pilot's Report

I climbed without incident to 6,000 feet where I was in and out of the cloud tops. About fifteen minutes into the flight, I noticed that the ammeter was discharging. I could not reestablish operation of the alternator. I contacted Center. I was given vectors to [an airport], cleared to descend to 2,100 feet, and cleared for a GPS approach. While making the procedure turn inbound, I began to experience icing, abandoned the approach, and climbed back to 6,000 feet. I requested to fly to [my original destination] where, hopefully, I would be able to do an ILS or surveillance approach. I informed Center that I would shut off all my electrical equipment to maintain as much battery power as possible. I continued to fly in the general direction of [my destination]... I turned the radio on and found that I had experienced a complete electrical failure.

I contacted Flight Service on my cell phone and then was given a number to contact Approach Control. The Controller informed me that I was 20 miles east of [an alternate airport] and suggested...that he could permit me to descend to 1,800 feet MSL. [The airport] was reporting a 1,800 foot overcast at that time. He gave me a vector to [the airport] and cleared me to descend to 1,800 feet. I broke out into the clear and, with the vector assistance, was able to land without incident.

NOTES:

MICROBURST ON RUNWAY 27 - B737

CALLBACK

Feb 2016, Issue 433, Captain's Report

During the approach we had visual contact with the airport. At about four miles the runway was in sight. There was no turbulence or rain. Tower advised that there was a microburst on Runway 27. About one mile out, we encountered moderate rain for about 15 seconds. I thought the previous aircraft had landed, so I continued as no turbulence or windshear conditions were being experienced... I elected to leave flaps at 15 degrees in case a go-around was conducted (normal landing is 30 degrees flaps). Just as I flared for landing, we began to experience a strong crosswind from the right.

The aircraft wanted to drift left during rollout. As we slowed, control was regained and we taxied off the runway to the ramp. Later, another company pilot (who was waiting for takeoff) told me that the preceding and following aircraft had gone around. As mentioned, I believed the preceding aircraft had landed. In hindsight, I should have gone around and waited for better weather conditions... This incident (although turning out OK) could have been serious... The safer course would have been to go around. I will not hesitate performing a go-around next time.

NOTES:

TOO LOW FLAPS - B737

CALLBACK

Feb 2016, Issue 433, Captain's Report

I turned off the autopilot/throttles as we intercepted LOC/glideslope and hand flew the aircraft. I called, "Gear down, Flaps 15." Under 170 knots, on glideslope and LOC, I called for Flaps 25. At approximately 1,500 feet and 163 knots I called, "Flaps 30, Landing checklist," but at the same time we experienced a gust and the First Officer hesitated due to our proximity to flap limit speed. He verbalized this and I acknowledged that I was slowing the aircraft. At this time there was a bright lightning strike just north of the field and several other flashes on both sides of the aircraft. There was also a radio transmission that interrupted us.

We had 12 knots of tailwind from 1,500 feet down to 800 feet and I was completely "outside" flying the aircraft, thinking windshear was possible and mentally prepping to execute a windshear recovery manoeuvre. I was focused on flying and landing on Runway 28. We started with light rain and as we approached the runway, rain increased to moderate, but the runway was in sight throughout. At approximately 400 feet AGL we got the caution, "Too low flaps," which startled us and I immediately looked at the flap indicator (at 25), then the gear (Down, three Green), and brakes (Armed, Green light).

I directed the First Officer to select Flaps 30 and do the Landing check. I said, "We are not going around in this weather for that; the weather is too bad." The First Officer agreed and selected Flaps 30. The radar was showing red in all forward directions, but we did not encounter windshear. We landed normally in the touchdown zone.

NOTES:

THE USUAL SUSPECTS - B737

CALLBACK

June 2016, Issue 437

The [destination station] Crew Chief came to the cockpit and inquired about how the aircraft handled during our flight....He then informed me that according to his paperwork all cargo should have been loaded in the aft compartment but, when opened, he found it completely empty. Upon further inspection he found that all cargo was loaded in the forward compartment. I checked my load planning paperwork and found the plan was for 1,900 pounds of cargo to be loaded in the aft compartment. Closeout paperwork showed 1,100 pounds of cargo with no indication whether forward or aft.

I then called Dispatch and was transferred to Load Planning. They checked the computer and said that all cargo should have been loaded in the aft compartment..., but that was not the case. Actual loading was in the forward compartment.

We had a light load of only 105 souls on board and a light cargo load. The Load Agent ran the numbers with the actual cargo in the forward compartment and found that we were still within safe CG limits. How much [mis-loaded] cargo weight would it have taken on this aircraft to create an unsafe situation? Would a full load of passengers have helped or hindered the situation? How about fuel burn on a long flight? Is it the Ground Crew's habit to load cargo in the forward [compartment] on smaller aircraft? Did they fall back on habit or disregard loading documents?

The load closeout we receive in the cockpit does not show forward or aft cargo weights. It just shows total weight and a breakdown for live animals and restricted articles. Maybe we should receive that information on closeout. Although that would not have helped in this situation since all the "paperwork" was correct.

NOTES:

TRUST, BUT VERIFY- B737-800

CALLBACK

June 2016, Issue 437

After the parking brake was released for push back, the Ground Crew opened the forward cargo door twice without notifying the Captain. The Captain flew to our destination and other than noting that the aircraft was nose heavy on takeoff, the flight was uneventful. After we parked, the Crew Chief entered the cockpit as the passengers were deplaning. He explained that the cargo had been incorrectly loaded and pointed to his offload report. The report clearly showed that only one bag should have been placed in the forward cargo and the rest should have been in the aft cargo. The Crew Chief reported that the aft cargo was empty and all the bags were in the forward cargo. Obviously this was a very serious issue, one that could have caused aircraft controllability issues, or worse... Pilots should have the same paperwork used to load the aircraft so we can double check with the load closeout and takeoff performance data and verify proper loading.

NOTES:

THE EDGE OF THE ENVELOPE - CRJ-700

CALLBACK

June 2016, Issue 437

Due to ACARS weight and balance, I directed the Ramp Lead to move the one and only bag from the aft cargo compartment to the front and to add 500 pounds of ballast to the front cargo compartment. On rotation we noticed a slight nose up pitch tendency, but dismissed it as normal for the aft CG limit. On arrival, the First Officer discovered that the 500 pounds of ballast had been placed in the aft cargo compartment.

NOTES:

LATE ARRIVALS - A319

CALLBACK

June 2016, Issue 437

We received a flow release time from ATC that was 10 minutes from our scheduled push time. At push we had not received the weights so I sent an ACARS [message] because I wanted to make sure we had the weights to make our slot time. I received the response that weights were not available because the ramp had not completed the loading document. We continued to taxi to the active runway where we held for 10 minutes waiting for weights and missed our slot time. I called Station Operations and they said they were talking to Load Planning about the weights. We waited another five minutes and received a Dispatch ACARS message stating our zero fuel weight had gone up 4,000 pounds with new [projected] fuel burn and fuel at touchdown numbers. We acknowledged the increase and accepted the numbers. The weight manifest printed and it showed our weight below the weight I had used to calculate performance numbers. After we departed, we received another weight manifest with an even lower gross weight and numbers closer to the planned weights on the flight plan. While the numbers we were working with resulted in minimal changes in the CG, there was potential for a very serious error to occur.

NOTES:

MISSING FROM THE MANIFEST

CALLBACK

June 2016, Issue 437

Upon arrival, this Air Carrier Flight Crew noticed three tires being offloaded, but had no paperwork or knowledge that they were even onboard during the flight.

From the First Officer's report:

The Captain and I, upon receiving the load sheet, asked the Ramp Agent if it was correct. We were told that it was. During the post flight inspection, I noticed Ground Operations removing three main tires from our [aft] baggage compartment. I did not remember seeing this on the load sheet, so I went back up to the cockpit and took [another] look at the load sheet. To my surprise there were no tires listed in the baggage compartment. We departed unaware that we had an extra 300 pounds of cargo in the back of the aircraft.

From the Captain's report:

During the post flight walk around, the First Officer noticed that three tires were being removed from the [aft] cargo bin. He asked the Ramp Agent if those were on our flight and he replied that they were. The First Officer got the cargo load report from the trash and it showed no cargo [listed] on the airplane other than the standard bags, the heavy checked bag and the gate claim items. Each tire weighs 100 pounds, so 300 pounds were missing from the cargo load report. We both agreed that missing items on the cargo load report was a safety of flight issue.

NOTES:

WHO'S ON FIRST - ERJ-170

CALLBACK

June 2016, Issue 437

The Ramp personnel asked the First Officer during his walk around if we could accommodate...freight weighing a total of approximately 2,000 pounds. He instructed them to wait on loading until he could confirm that the load could be safely accommodated. When the First Officer returned to the ramp, the cargo was already loaded in the aft compartment and he was told it was approximately 1,000 pounds. When we received the cargo load report, it indicated a total load of 59 standard and 5 heavy bags in forward cargo and 1,000 pounds of freight loaded in the aft cargo compartment. We ran the reported load and after reseating four passengers as a result, we received good takeoff performance numbers. After closing the door, the tug driver said they had made a mistake and that we should add 1 standard bag to the forward compartment and that the actual weight in the rear was 2,200 pounds. I asked twice to clarify these numbers, but I wasn't confident in his count. We ran new numbers anyway and adjusted the passengers, once again, per the ACARS instruction.

I called Ops before taxiing to confirm the load numbers. The

Ramp Manager told me that the second numbers I had received were, in fact, accurate. Just prior to reaching the runway, we received a message from Dispatch stating to once again add two bags to the forward cargo. After a normal takeoff and being airborne for approximately 30 minutes, Dispatch informed us that the load in the rear cargo compartment was actually 4,000 pounds. The cargo compartment's weight limitation was exceeded.... They [then] informed me that the CG was out of limits and...the decision was made to divert. After a 74,000 pound uneventful landing, Ramp personnel removed and weighed all cargo from both front and rear compartments. The actual contents of both compartments were: 62 standard and 4 heavy [bags] forward, and 3,600 pounds in the rear compartment.

NOTES:

FREIGHT FORWARD - ATR-72-212

CASA

May 2015

Many years ago I was employed in Asia flying an ATR-72-212. This aircraft has a gross weight of 22,000kg and carries 72 passengers and two cabin and two tech crew. This day's flying involved four sectors starting and ending at our home base. It was the monsoon season and the weather forecast indicated bad weather and minimums all round.

The first three sectors went without incident; however, the take-off for the final sector was a bit different than expected. We had boarded the passengers, and our ground weight was around 20,000kg from memory. This was on the limit for this airfield, which was about 5000 ft AMSL, slightly undulating, narrow by most standards and had piles of gravel laid all around the runway ready for building a new runway at some future stage.

After receiving the manifest and load and trim sheet, the first officer and I examined it together, set the trim for take-off, set the V speeds and when the door was closed, we fired up the left engine. (The right engine was running with the prop brake on to provide power for the lighting etc. on board.)

I taxied out and lined up after having briefed the F/O on the take-off. I then opened the throttles and pushed them forward into the take-off detent. (In the detent, you have set 90 per cent power which is enough for the take-off).

The aircraft accelerated and at 110 kt the F/O called 'rotate'. I eased the control back, but nothing happened. I immediately looked at the ASI to see if I had set the bugs correctly. (The bugs are three different-coloured plastic markers which you set manually on the outer rim of the ASI: the first one to denote V1, the second Vr and the third V2 which are the reference speed which must be achieved for the take-off and initial climb.)

At the time, all company pilots were flying around 120 hours per month. We had been doing this for some time, so we were all suffering from chronic fatigue. The aviation laws in this country did not have any rules for duty time, so we were worked pretty hard.

One manifestation of chronic fatigue was for the pilots to set the bugs 10 kt slow—never fast, just slow. The strange thing was that the captain and the first officer would do this; and even after cross-checking each other's settings, would both declare they were set correctly, even when they were 10 kt slow. This was common to all crews.

As I had determined that the rotate speed was set correctly, my immediate thoughts were that I had an elevator control unlock—you can unlock the elevator in this aircraft if it is stuck. I pulled the control back until it hit the limiting stop; still nothing happened.

We were accelerating very rapidly by this time. There was precious little runway left and the thought of going off the end of the runway and impacting the gravel piles in a country that did not have pethidine or morphine did not appeal to me.

In an emergency in the ATR, you can push the throttles out of the 90 per cent detent up to a stop at the 100 per cent position; and if needed, in the case of windshear and microbursts, you can push them further to the 115 per cent position. When you do this, you feel the throttles start to rise as you have to push them up a ramp. It is designed that way so you know what you are doing without looking at the throttle position, to prevent inadvertent excessive power demands.

When you do this you will cause excessive turbine rub and basically when you land you will need to overhaul the engines—so, not a good career move.

As the aircraft did not rotate, the only thing I could think of was to get more air over the elevators, so I pushed the throttles forward and told the first officer I was going 'up the ramp', so he knew I was going to apply maximum power available.

I felt the power levers hit the 100 per cent position and start to rise up the ramp. Just as I had pushed them up a small amount, the nose slowly started to rise so I took my hand off the throttles and held the control full back. The power levers fell back to the 100 per cent position.

Just after lift-off I felt a small shudder which I guess was the main wheels hitting one of the gravel piles off the end of the runway.

As the aircraft accelerated I started easing the control forward and trimming the aircraft back. Normally the trim will sit at 1.0 or 1.2 rear for the take-off which is what was set; however, as we accelerated, I kept trimming back until the trim hit the 4.5 maximum rear position.

We carried out the usual after take-off procedures and when complete the first officer said, 'thank God that's over with'. I said 'it isn't over yet as I am not sure I can flare the aircraft for the landing'.

The en-route part of the flight was uneventful. However, when we were cleared for the ILS 30nm from the field, I began experimenting with speeds to see what speed was needed to give me sufficient control authority to flare for the landing.

The speed was about 170 kt (normally about 135 kt) and after checking the bible it was above the brake energy limits and tyre speed limits for the aircraft, again not a good prospect.

We proceeded with the ILS and fortunately broke visual about 800 ft AGL and I picked up the PAPI (visual precision approach path indicator for landings) and maintained a normal approach profile at the higher speed to about 200ft AGL. I then allowed the aircraft to get low on the PAPI as I was trying to flatten the approach to reduce the flare on landing.

The touchdown went well and the tyres held together. After deceleration to normal speeds I applied reverse thrust, then brakes, and taxied in to the terminal.

When we had parked, I asked the first officer to go and tell the baggage handlers not to take the bags and freight to the terminal, as I wanted to inspect them first. After completing the (post-flight) cockpit duties I proceeded to the baggage trolleys and escorted them to the terminal. I made the ground crew weigh all items.

The result? Eight hundred kilograms of freight manifested for the rear cargo hold had been placed in the forward cargo hold. There was very little freight in the rear hold.

I might point out that neither the first officer or myself checked the bags and freight after loading. We had qualified loadmasters who took care of all this, and it was not company policy for the tech crew to check where the freight was. We could have checked it visually, but not knowing what the items weighed, it would have been impossible to know if there was a problem.

After the engineers had downloaded the flight parameters to their laptop, they advised me that no engine damage had occurred. Apparently I had powered up to about 103 per cent and only for a couple of seconds, so all was well. And there was no apparent damage to the undercarriage from the impact after take-off.

The loadmaster responsible for the loading had his employment opportunities immediately freed up.

When an aircraft is loaded so far out of C of G you generally get really bad control problems, which can have catastrophic consequences—however, the ATR flew like a dream even with the C of G substantially out of position. This is a great testimony to the designers and builders of this aircraft.

I have submitted this article as food for thought for my colleagues currently flying—it is an emergency that just 'doesn't happen'. It did to me. Makes you think doesn't it?

NOTES:

EARLY DESCENT

CALLBACK

May 2016, Issue 436

While diverting to an alternate, I received the ATIS and was being vectored for the ILS. After receiving a clearance for the approach, the Controller explained that he had just come on duty and was not aware that the glideslope was out of service. He apologized and amended my clearance to the LOC approach. I don't remember the specific ceiling being reported, but I asked if anyone had made it in on the Localizer since I was thinking that the weather was too low. He checked with the Tower and replied, "Yes." I accepted the clearance for the LOC, but with all the radio transmissions and cockpit distractions, I never gave myself time to "brief the approach."

As soon as I was established, I started down to my first step down fix. Problem was, I was still outside the Final Approach Fix. I never received a TAWS (Terrain Awareness and Warning System) Alert, but realized my mistake when I received a "Terrain Alert" from my Number 2 NavCom. I arrested my descent and in doing so, the Alert went away. I had a "holy [cow]" moment, realizing what I had done and my potentially fatal CFIT situation. At that point I continued on the approach and, being in shock over the mistake I had just made, missed my next and final step down fix to the MDA. As I continued to the Missed Approach Point there was a small break in the overcast, but being high and in no place to make a stabilized approach to landing, I executed and reported "missed approach" to the Tower. They handed me back to TRACON and I was vectored to the ILS for another runway which concluded in a normal approach and landing.

While I found no unusual hazards in my "Preflight Risk Assessment," it is apparent that my lack of familiarity with my destination airport combined with the lack of time for an approach briefing led to a lack of situational awareness in the approach procedure. In hindsight, better CRM may have included asking for vectors to come around again to intercept the final approach course, which would have allowed time for an appropriate approach briefing. Never again!

NOTES:

FROM COMPLACENCY TO CRISIS

CALLBACK

May 2016, Issue 436

An M20 was en route at 9,000 feet, west to east. A CRJ200 was a departure off Runway 11. Traffic was slow and I was only controlling four planes. I established radar contact with the CRJ200 on departure and put him on course. The CRJ200 was climbing out of about 4,000 feet when I switched him to Center. At the time, the conflict with the 9,000 foot overflight M20 was about 15 to 20 miles away and I did not see it. I saw the conflict when the aircraft were about six to seven miles apart and opposite direction to each other. I called to the aircraft I was talking to (the M20) and told him to turn right heading 180 immediately and then gave him the traffic call. I did not wait for the response and called Center and said to turn the CRJ200 north. Both aircraft were on east/west lines opposite direction to each other. The CRJ200 was heading 270; the M20 heading 090. I again called the M20 to turn right heading 180 immediately with no response. I made the call again, no response. Then the M20 called and said, "Are you calling me?" and I realized I had been using the wrong callsign. The callsign had a "W" and I had been calling "M." The aircraft passed clear thanks to TCAS and a RA alert.

This near midair was completely my fault. I was complacent and focused on the departure aircraft. I gave him the same thing we always give them. The slowness of the position and routine of the departure lulled me into a false sense of awareness. I have [many] years of ATC experience and this goes to show you can never let your guard down. If TCAS had not been on the aircraft, the outcome could have been catastrophic. I have learned from this error and will be forever diligent. Never again!

NOTES:

DOWN TO THE LAST DROP

CASA

Name withheld by request, Mar 9, 2017

It was early autumn many years ago and I was scheduled to fly a freight charter from Sydney airport to several airports north returning to Bankstown in the afternoon. The flight was one I had done many times before and this one was shaping up to be 'just another day at the office'. Even the weather was cooperating—fine with no holding or alternates required. I carried out my pre-flight checks which included checking the fuel quantity.

In the 58 Baron there are two fuel tanks—one in each wing feeding their respective engines. Cross-feed and off can also be selected. The fuel capacity of each tank is quite generous but restricts the payload if filled to full. As most flights were normally of short duration, we rarely needed full tanks. To determine the amount of fuel in the tanks we kept a paper-based fuel log and, just to be sure the log was accurate, we also filled up to full every Monday morning as a cross-check when the outbound payload was minimal.

Shortly before my incident a decision had been made to carry additional freight on Monday mornings. But full tanks plus the extra cargo would exceed the maximum take-off weight. So we no longer filled to full on Mondays, just occasionally when we had an ad-hoc charter or required holding or alternate fuel. As a result, we now relied almost entirely on a paper-based system and the fuel gauges.

The fuel gauges, like many GA aircraft, seemed to be vaguely accurate on the ground but once in the air they jumped around in turbulence and changes in aircraft attitude. There was also another issue with this particular Baron. The electrical system worked properly but occasionally it did strange things. I once pushed the test button for the ILS marker beacons—they worked—but it also disconnected the autopilot!

Another time, climbing out of Sydney, the fuel gauges suddenly dropped to zero. It was far too rapid even for a massive fuel leak but I glanced back over the wings anyway. Nothing. The engines kept running. I changed frequency to the 'chit-chat channel' and told one of the other pilots what had just happened. In a calm voice, he told me to switch to the other voltage regulator. I threw the switch and the fuel gauges quickly rose up from empty and returned to somewhere around three-quarters full again. Go figure.

So on this morning, I really only had the paper-based fuel log to rely on. And perhaps one other method. All pilots have removed the fuel caps and peered into the tanks looking for fuel. In the 58 Barons you could only see the fuel when the tanks were almost full. But if you grabbed the wing and 'shook' it, you could hear the fuel sloshing around inside the tank. A crude confirmation of the fuel quantity.

I removed the cap, looked in and saw nothing. I shook the wing. To my surprise I heard a distant sloshing of fuel rather than a 'fuller' sound. Not really what I expected or had heard on other flights when I knew I had sufficient fuel. I remember being puzzled by this so I retrieved the fuel log to check the amount of fuel that should have been on board. The fuel log showed I had more than enough for the proposed flights. Despite the quietly ringing alarm bells in my head, I secured the fuel caps and completed the pre-flight. The outbound flights that morning were normal and routine.

After spending the day at a hotel I prepared the aircraft for the afternoon return flight to Bankstown via one en-route stop. The fuel 'slosh test' sounded even more distant but the fuel log said it was OK. The intermediate landing and departure went well and soon I was in cruise at 4000 feet for the final leg to Bankstown. Our autopilots usually didn't work so I was hand-flying it, on top of a broken under-cast in smooth air with a slowly setting sun to the west. I sat back, looked at the instrument panel and admired how good everything looked: power set, mixtures leaned, altitude nailed, on track, on time ... then I saw the EGT needle on the right engine suddenly drop.

The engine started to surge and the aircraft yawed as the power fluctuated. I started to go through the engine failure drill from memory but I quickly realised it was a fuel problem. I changed the fuel selector to cross-feed from the other tank and flicked the fuel pump to 'low'. The surging and yawing stopped and the engine resumed normal power again. Everything flashed through my mind in rapid succession—if both tanks have theoretically the same amount of fuel and one has just run dry, the other can't be far behind. And by running both engines off one tank I was consuming fuel at double the rate from a fuel tank that must be close to empty.

Below me was 'tiger country' and I couldn't see any suitable landing sites if both engines failed completely. Just trees. I had to keep flying. But how could I squeeze every drop out of the tank. We normally operated at a relatively high power setting—speed was more important than range or economy. A lower power setting would deliver more 'bang for my fuel buck' although at a lower speed. I throttled back to 65 per cent power and re-leaned.

Another pilot once told me how when flying a different model Baron—the B55—which had auxiliary tanks, he could 'milk' as much as 10 minutes of extra fuel out of a seemingly empty auxiliary tank by switching back to it every few minutes. I switched to the dry tank to pick up any dregs of fuel in it. It worked, the engine kept running smoothly for about five minutes. Then the engine started to surge and fail. Back to cross-feed. I did this perhaps four or five times, each time

I got less and less fuel until finally, as soon as I switched tanks, the engine would fail. The empty tank really was empty now.

I crossed the Hawkesbury River and soon Westmead came into sight. I copied the ATIS and called the tower. I knew I couldn't afford to fly a circuit. Mercifully, runway 11 was in use and I was given circuit entry instructions to join on left base.

I lowered the gear and the first stage of flap. I decided to wait until I had the runway made before taking the final stage of flap. I also made my approach a bit high, just in case. I started my turn onto final. But every time I banked left the fuel pick-up would unport and the right engine would start to fail. When I rolled wings level, the engine ran smooth. So to complete my turn on to final I did a series of small banks, wings level, small bank, wings level. I can still see in my mind's eye the image of the runway on final. I was quite high but I had made it. Full flap. Close the throttles. I landed and taxied clear.

But it was a close-run thing. As I was turning onto the parallel taxiway both engines started spluttering. I hit the fuel pumps. No good, both engines clattered to a stop. I can still hear the whine of the fuel pumps normally inaudible over the sound of the engines. I switched everything off and called for the fuel truck.

ATSB and CASA publications contain some excellent information. But they also acknowledge there are limitations with dipsticks, sight gauges, drip gauges, tank tabs, electrical gauges and visual indications of fuel. In my case, all were either not available or subject to error. Couldn't happen to you? Hopefully it never does. The ATSB notes 49 lives lost in a nine-year period due to fuel problems. It's far better to have a good 'hangar story' than a good obituary.

NOTES:

THE RULE OF THREE

CASA

Name withheld by request, Jan 13, 2016

I spent my childhood dreaming of becoming a pilot and getting paid to do something I loved so much. I was working in my first job, with a fresh commercial pilot's licence, full of enthusiasm, a desire to do well and progress in my career. I was operating a Cessna 206 for a charter company in the top end of Australia, working to support people living in isolated communities.

I follow a rule of thumb when operating day VFR—there are three major variables to work with: light, fuel and weather. If you have plenty of two of these variables, you can operate to a lower margin with the remaining one. For example, on a short morning flight with full tanks, you can accept non-CAVOK (ceiling and visibility okay) but VMC conditions, but I wouldn't accept the same flight if it was going to push last-light margins. This is a story about the time that I let commercial pressures get in the way of my personal margins, and learnt the value of boundaries the hard way.

It was mid-wet season in the top end, and we had been experiencing some monsoonal weather patterns. One Friday afternoon I was tasked to pick up passengers from three different communities and bring them into 'town' so that they could catch the scheduled flight to Darwin that evening. The weather had been pretty good for VFR that day, but at that time of year there is a high probability of afternoon thunderstorms. I was also at the end of my duty cycle and approaching my hour limits.

I fuelled up with more fuel than required for legal margins, as I had a rough idea of my expected payload and performance requirements for the flight. The first two pick-ups went fine, but en route to the final pick-up a large band of weather started to approach my destination, which to a seasoned top-end pilot would have been expected. Checking my watch, I figured I could spare 25–30 minutes for delays and still be able to make it back to base with enough time before last light, as well as being able to hold for 60 minutes as the current TEMPOs required.

I could see the strip as I flew abeam it, and I decided the weather was still a while away. I decided I had time to get in and get out before the weather arrived. It was at this point my passengers already on board reminded me of the reservations they had for their scheduled flight to Darwin that evening. More pressure.

I landed on the shortish gravel strip. This one has a three per cent gradient up until the middle, and then slopes back down. It has 700 metre usable, with tall trees at either end. I made the landing without issue, and parked to retrieve my final passenger for the day.

The passenger decided that he wasn't going to travel unless his brother and children could come too. As I already had three passengers on board, and because of the restrictive length of the strip, I was unable to accept this payload. A discussion ensued ... my precious time was running out. The weather was also getting closer. We could now see lightning and the delay to the thunderclap was getting shorter. We needed to depart, and soon, or we would all be staying— no-one would be catching their flight that night. More pressure. The difficult passenger decided to stay behind—a decision that I believe later saved us from having a much more dire outcome.

I got the passengers back into the plane, briefed them, fired up the engine and began my backtrack to the end of the runway. I checked the windsock as we taxied past: it was a quartering 10 kt headwind from my left for take-off. I completed the rest of my checks as we backtracked, gave myself a take-off safety brief as was standard procedure, and nominated a safe abort point. At this critical phase, I was starting to rush, and it was starting to rain. I swung the 206 around, firewalled the throttle and accelerated up the hill. I was protected from the wind because of the trees, but the acceleration was as expected and normal.

The crest of the strip blocks your view of the windsock from the threshold. We accelerated to take-off speed, rotated and became airborne. Soon after passing my safe abort point I called 'Continue'. We weren't climbing much past 50 ft. As we passed the windsock, I glanced at it. We now had a quartering tailwind. In my rush to get away, I had under-estimated the effects of the approaching weather, and we were running out of space quickly. I tried turning slightly away from the full tail wind, and waited for what seemed like forever for the aircraft to accelerate and climb. We cleared the trees at the end, but only by a margin that was well below what I consider comfortable!

The flight continued without event after that, if not a bit quieter in the cabin than usual. Everyone made their flight and I got home, but not without learning a very valuable lesson that I take with me every time I fly.

On that day, I let the pressure to succeed get to me. I was trying to please my boss and meet the expectations of the passengers who wanted to make their flight that night. I'll admit my own personal pressure to perform pushed me as well. Giving into the pressure almost cost us all very dearly. I'm now very strict with myself with my rule of three variables. The day that I pushed two of them was almost my last. I learnt the value of not rushing, of making all checks purposefully and methodically. I also discovered how fast the wind can change!

NOTES:

CHAPTER 4

COMMUNICATION & AIR CREW

"Mix ignorance with arrogance at low altitude and the results are almost guaranteed to be spectacular."
Bruce Landsberg
Executive Director
AOPA Air Safety Foundation.

AN AIR CARRIER'S PREMATURE PUSHBACK

CALLBACK

Jan 2017, Issue 444

At the same time we were cleared to push, we received a [third] message for inaccurate weights. I told the push crew that we needed to get new weights before we pushed. We got new weights and loaded them into the FMC. When cleared to push, I released the brakes and said, "Brakes released, cleared to push, disconnect abeam gate XX." We started moving, but no verbal response was heard from the push crew. After trying to contact [the push crew] on the headset, the aircraft stopped. I still thought we had a communication problem. One of the wing walkers got on the headset and told us there was no one in the tug.

NOTES:

FROM DEFECT TO CONFLICT AND COMPLEXITY

CALLBACK

Jan 2017, Issue 444

[The airport] was running an east operation, and we were on approach for Runway XX. We were given vectors to turn north for the base leg and 3,000 feet. I had spotted the preceding aircraft, as well as the aircraft on approach for Runway YY. Approach called us and issued a right turn to a heading of 070. I sensed everything went quiet because usually there is a bit more with that clearance, so I looked at [the] radio and realized that Communication Radio 1 was transmitting. We had a stuck microphone, yet as I scanned all the switches, none were in the [Radio Transmit (R/T)] position. The First Officer (FO) and I both [realized the condition] at the same time, and [we] began checking our switches more thoroughly. The FO was the Pilot Flying (PF), and as we were converging with traffic from the adjacent runway, coupled with a small delay caused by our becoming aware of the malfunction, he elected to disengage the autopilot to expedite the turn back toward our localizer. Additionally, because we had strayed and it appeared that the adjacent aircraft had started a descent based on our TCAS, [the FO] started a shallow descent as well.

Once we established a heading back toward our approach course and were no longer in unsafe proximity of the Runway YY approach course, we levelled off. To make matters worse during this situation, we didn't realize for a few moments that he and I couldn't hear one another over the crew intercom, and the FO is hearing impaired. We were both talking, thinking the other person could hear, and at one point, he asked me to take the controls so he could investigate his headphone jacks, but I didn't hear him. Nothing came of that because he was only a moment in doing so, but under a different set of circumstances there could have been very different results. I didn't think there was a procedure in the QRH for our situation and felt that what little time I had to correct this problem without it escalating into an even bigger problem was best spent trying to [troubleshoot] a couple of things I knew of from basic system knowledge. I isolated the [communication radios] by selecting EMERG on both [audio control panels], and it solved the problem. Although the FO could not hear ATC or me, I was able reestablish communication with the Approach Controller and obtain proper clearances. As we crossed the outer marker, ATC issued a low altitude alert as a result of the descent manoeuvre we performed earlier. We had levelled off at 2,200 feet, and ATC advised us that the minimum altitude at the outer marker was 2,700 feet. We established the aircraft on the glideslope and continued to a normal landing. The FO's [communication radios] came back somewhere along the approach but went back out during taxi in. We reported to ground control that we were having problems with the radios, and we were extra vigilant during taxi in.

The biggest threat was losing communication with ATC at a very critical phase of the approach, in very congested and busy airspace.... The nature of this malfunction didn't allow a determination of the full scope of debilitation immediately; it became a huge distraction when coupled with the tight constraints of the operating environment. The idea of flying in such busy, complex airspace without [communication, and thereby] imperilling one's own aircraft as well as others, caused extreme pressure to correct the issue.

NOTES:

IMPAIRED CREW
COMMUNICATIONS

CALLBACK

Jan 2017, Issue 444

The first attempt to land...was unsuccessful due to fog, and the flight returned to [the departure airport]. The flight then changed Captains and was re-dispatched.... The [second] Captain was on his second day of being [assigned involuntary flying] and [had been] pulled off his deadhead aircraft home to [fly this] turn... He was understandably upset and was having problems hearing the First Officer (FO) through the [communications system], since there was no HOT MIC function on this [aircraft]. Unfortunately this was not identified until the return trip. The Captain missed several CRM calls from the FO on climb out, and the FO assumed it was due to his emotional state, but it was also due to the [communications system issue]. Upon approach to [the airport], Approach Control vectored the flight to a position north of [the airport] and asked if they had the field in sight. [The destination] recently had a snow and frost event, and the Crew was having problems identifying the field. Everything looked white. The Captain responded that they had it; the FO concurred and began to manoeuvre for landing. At approximately 1,300 feet AGL, both pilots noted that the runway did not line up with the navaids and verbalized, "This doesn't look right." At that time, [the] Tower informed the Crew that they were lined up on the wrong airfield. A go-around was conducted, the flight manoeuvred for the proper airfield, and [we] landed uneventfully.

NOTES:

DISPATCH ISOLATION

CALLBACK

Jan 2017, Issue 444

As I was building the release for this flight, I was getting an error that [indicated] the drift-down alternates could not be calculated because of an error. [A fellow Dispatcher] told me to file it and make sure that the drift-down information was on the release. I filed it and checked the release, but the [drift-down] information was missing. After I corrected this issue, I called [the associated ARTCC] to pull the flight strip, sent the corrected [flight plan], sent an ACARS message to the crew, and then called Ops to pass the information to the crew to print the new [flight plan]. While the flight was en route, I got a message from the crew that the route given to them by ATC was not matching what was on the release. I sent [the crew] the corrected flight summary, the drift-down information, and the weather for [their] escape airport. I then did a pen and ink for the new flight plan. The Captain said he was not notified by the gate agent and did not receive [my] ACARS [message].

There was a breakdown of communication. The gate agent did

not notify the crew to print the new [flight plan], and the crew did not receive the ACARS message. The next time I [will] directly call the Captain and follow up to ensure that they have the correct [flight plan].

NOTES:

CONTROLLER PILOT DATA LINK COMMUNICATIONS INTRODUCTION

CALLBACK

Controller Pilot Data Link Communication Departure Clearance Services (CPDLC-DCL) is one segment of the Future Air Navigation System (FANS) that has been recently implemented in the contiguous 48 states at local Tower Data Link Service (TDLS) equipped facilities to deliver departure clearances and revised departure clearances prior to takeoff.

As any new system is implemented, some "bugs" may be expected, and CPDLC-DCL is no exception. There are reports suggesting that crews are experiencing problems while using CPDLC-DCL for its intended objective. The problems that are experienced point to sources from system architecture, to precise meanings of specific words and formats used in the CPDLC-DCL syntax, to basic interpretation and understanding of the CPDLC-DCL information protocols and operational procedures.

The following reports are incidents of complications that arose from the crews' use of CPDLC-DCL to obtain departure clearances and revised departure clearances.

CAUTIOUS PILOT DISTRUSTS LINK COMMUNICATIONS

CALLBACK

Dec 2016, Issue 443

During preflight, we received a revised clearance via CPDLC. The change was from the TRALR6.DVC to the STAAV6.DVC. I verified [the] clearance and received a full route clearance over the radio. When the LOAD feature was selected in CPDLC, the new revised route did not LOAD into the ROUTE page properly. It still showed [the] TRALR6.DVC, but now it had a discontinuity. At this point, I had to load the route manually. When I did load the STAAV SIX, however, I failed to select the DVC transition, [so the FMC] now had point STAAV direct to LAA in the LEGS page. When we did the route verification later, during the preflight, we both failed to detect the missing transition that included the points TRALR, NICLE, and DVC.

This went unnoticed until passing point STAAV on the departure. That is when ATC queried us if we were headed to point TRALR. We indicated to ATC that we were direct LAA. He recleared us to TRALR to resume the departure. There was nothing significant to report for the rest of the flight.

After using CPDLC to obtain their clearance, this Air Carrier Crew saw no indications that their clearance had been revised. It appeared the same as the filed route, so they did not LOAD it. ATC soon called them off course.

Prior to departing SNA we loaded the FMC using normal procedures.... We received a ready prompt but did not get a clearance. Shortly before push we still had not received a CPDLC clearance, so we requested a clearance via PDC. We got a PDC reply message stating to use CPDLC, and simultaneously a clearance was uploaded to the FMC ATC page. The clearance showed our departure and transition as filed, as well as the altitude restrictions, expected altitude, squawk, and departure frequencies as we expected to see. The ATC page did not state that it was a revised clearance or route. All obvious indications were [that] our clearance was unchanged from the filed route. A LOAD prompt and ACCEPT prompt were shown. We ACCEPTED the clearance, but because we had already loaded the flight plan, we did not LOAD the flight plan sent via CPDLC.

We departed as normal. Once airborne passing 10,000 feet, we received an ACARS flight progress print out that showed our originally filed course. After passing TRM, ATC stated they showed us off course. They gave us a revised route clearance.... There was no print out of our clearance to reference, and since the CPDLC did not display the full route clearance, we had difficulty tracking down whether or not there was actually a change to our originally filed route. We were able to find a LOAD prompt on page 3 of the ATC clearance page. When we selected LOAD, a new route was LOADED to the FMC, which was different from our originally filed route. We discovered our route had, in fact, been changed via CPDLC. We erased the change since we already had a new route assigned by ATC airborne and continued uneventfully to [our destination].

NOTES:

COMPLEX PRESENTATION —
DESIRED LEARNING CUMBERSOME

CALLBACK

Dec 2016, Issue 443

We received our departure clearance via CPDLC. During my preflight, I loaded the FMC with the route we were given on our release paperwork (PORTT THREE DEPARTURE). Our release had the following FMS route: KEWR BIGGY PTW J48 BYRDD J230 SAAME STEVY HVQ UNCKL MAUDD4 KSDF. When it came time to log on to the CPDLC, the Captain and I received the following [departure clearance]: CLEARED ROUTE CLEARANCE ORIGIN: KEWR DEST:KSDF ARRIVAL: DARBY 5.UNCKL +LOAD NEW RTE TO KSDF+ EWR2, CLB VIA SID EXC MAINT 2500FT EXPECT FL340 10 MIN AFT DP, DPFRQ 119.2 SQUAWK 1534, CTC GROUND 121.8 FOR TAXI.

When we saw that this was a change, I manually changed the SID to the NEWARK TWO off of Runway 22R. I did not select the LOAD prompt as I did not see any other change to our clearance. I believed our clearance was now the NEWARK TWO (flown in LNAV), and our first fix was still BIGGY then PTW, etc. The

Captain and I agreed on this. I printed the CPDLC clearance, folded it, and laid it on the centre console.

After takeoff, we were handed off to Departure Control. He cleared us to fly directly to a fix which neither the Captain nor I saw on our route. He said, "Don't you have the PARKE J6" on your routing. We said, "Negative, we have BIGGY PTW J48." He then just told us to fly a heading. He came back a short time after that and told us to fly directly to LRP and join J6 and expect a further clearance later. He did come back shortly thereafter, and told us to fly J6 to UNCKL, then the arrival....We obviously knew we had been expecting something different than the Controller had been, so I picked up the "printed" copy of the CPDLC clearance we had received, and on it was also the following: PARKE J6 UNCKL Note that this was NOT on the original CPDLC clearance we looked at on the FMC. I don't know if it had been truncated off due to space, or it had been inadvertently left off or what, but we both went back and looked and noticed this. That was why we thought the only change to our clearance was to the NEWARK TWO, [while keeping] the same fixes as we originally had on our paperwork (i.e. BIGGY PTW J48).

Contributing factors to this confusing situation are numerous. I now know that I am supposed to select the LOAD prompt when we have a change to our routing.... The method we are transitioning into with respect to getting our clearances via CPDLC is very confusing. The wording... on the FMC is not intuitive, and the overall procedure...is very convoluted.... We now receive our clearances in several different ways, at different airports, and in different airplanes, [which] all lead to a higher chance of mistakes.

NOTES:

COMPLICATED PROCESS DESTINES LOWERED COGNIZANCE

CALLBACK

Dec 2016, Issue 443

This CPDLC message arrived at precisely the wrong time. The Crew's attention was diverted, and their situational awareness suffered as they attempted to eliminate the confusion generated when they could not quickly resolve the revised clearance CPDLC message.

We were taxiing out of a very congested, weather-impacted, JFK airport the other day. The ground frequency was non-stop due to long taxi routes because of 20 mile in-trail spacing for departing aircraft in all directions. A CPDLC message [reading] "THIS IS A REVISED CLEARANCE" appeared with no other information. No revised route [was] included. [We] spent [the] next 5 to 10 minutes heads down, while taxiing, trying to figure out what was happening, in addition to eventually calling Clearance Delivery on the radio, and Dispatch. [There was] no place to pull out of [the] way due to long taxiways with no exits. And, we were getting automatic ACARS messages [that we] must be airborne in 15 minutes due to [the] 9 hour flight time restriction. A simple printout of the revised clearance would have resolved the issue in a few moments and would have been much more intuitive....

The current system of having an ATC clearance, current or revised, stored on multiple, disjointed pages of the ACARS or FMS display is confusing and causes excessive heads down time while taxi-ing. It will cause a gross navigational error,...is a defective system, and is going to harm someone.

NOTES:

COMMON PRECAUTIONS DEMYSTIFY LINK CONFUSION - B737

CALLBACK

Dec 2016, Issue 443

This B737 Captain was distracted with his wing anti-ice configuration during takeoff. The result was unintentional, but a significant deviation to the takeoff procedure occurred.

The First Officer loaded [the filed route] into the FMC before requesting a CPDLC clearance. The clearance came back, "CLEARED ROUTE CLEARANCE. FREE TEXT. POM9.GMN. FREE TEXT CLB VIA SID EXC MAINT 14000FT." The First Officer noticed a LOAD prompt, and [saw that] the new route [read], "DIRECT GMN DIRECT RGOOD RGOOD.EMZOH3.SKIZM." Because we were now confused, we called Clearance to see if we were now filed direct to GMN, but they cleared up our confusion. We were still on the POM9.GMN.

NOTES:

WHEN WORDS FAIL

CASA

Name withheld by request, Mar 28, 2014

'*Turn left heading xxx.*' The hair stood up on the back of my neck and an alarm bell rang in my head. The heading bore no resemblance to our track as our HS125 climbed through the lower levels to our cruising flight level on a cloudless and clear tropical morning on the company's daily commute carrying executives and engineers.

We had left a secondary airport some 15 miles southeast of a major capital city airport. Both were dispatching aircraft to the west and our track after a short climb straight ahead turned us right to track direct to the capital city VOR, and thence en route northbound with an unrestricted climb and a frequency transfer to the departures controller.

'*Turn left heading xxx.*' The heading was all wrong but, more than that, the controller's voice seemed to have gone up an octave. I thought I could detect some uncertainty and a hint of fear in his voice and at this stage of our flight it could only mean one thing, avoidance. I called it as 'traffic on the right, close!' simultaneously disengaging the autopilot, and after a quick glance outside rolled into a 45-degree bank to the left, as the first officer's head snapped to the side window, straining to catch a glimpse of the cause of the conflict. In broken accented English his voice, courtesy of the hot microphone system, said that he couldn't see anything—not surprising given our bank angle.

Then he shrieked. It was ear piercing. Incoherent words sounded through the headset, and my head spun to see that he was looking past me with his eyes wide, and open-mouthed trying to form words and gesticulating wildly.

My head snapped back and I leaned forward in my seat to see past the left windshield corner post. The DC-9 was climbing and was close, very close. It was large and gun barrel straight and it didn't move in my sight. I can remember being intrigued that I couldn't see past it, as it appeared to be emerging from a desert mirage, in a billowing heat haze generated by the engines. Our steep turn was keeping us a stationary target, like a bird and a hunter's buckshot converging in space.

I wrenched the rams-horn control column to bring the wings level and the nose up. My head swivelled to follow the DC-9's progress as it passed below and slightly behind, having never deviated in its flight path, climbing directly into the dazzling morning sun. I could plainly see the pilots' brilliant white shirts and sun-glassed faces, an image which in later years would remind me of a Gary Larsen 'Far Side' cartoon that still makes me uncomfortable when I see it.

The controller enquired if we were clear of traffic, instructed us to resume tracking and then passed us to the en-route frequency. Before we changed, we heard the radio erupting into the national language between the controller and the DC-9.

Was the incoherent shriek that had rung through my headphones and initiated the avoidance action miscommunication? Definitely not, the urgency, the direction of the threat and the adrenalin were all there, and although English was not the first officer's first language, his reaction was unambiguous, and was far more eloquent than words could ever be. Even though hardly a coherent word had been spoken,

it was the tone—from the initial heading instruction to the first officer's shriek—that gave all the communication life and urgency. Fright
played a major role.

The cockpit is an unnatural environment from a communication
standpoint. It's side-by-side, forward-facing and often widely sepa-
rated seating arrangement is less than conducive to the flow of information. It can make the disembodied spoken word, in isolation, very
fragile, and often has a high ambient noise level. Messages tend to be
stripped, prefabricated and presented in a dry unemotional manner
across the void, and the response is equally clipped.

My flight school lecturer used to say that if cockpits were about
communication they would be crewed by two women and have a
coffee table layout, where every word, tone and expression, as well as
the body language of the speaker, could be assessed for its urgency,
import or otherwise. It's why we lean together or turn to face each
other when there is something important to say or hear, so that we are
better able to digest and understand it. But in the cockpit we look out
of the windscreen.

A later review of the airport SIDs as to how an aircraft would
appear from that quadrant showed it had departed the capital city
airport on a climbing right teardrop to the northeast to bring it back
overhead the VOR for a departure to the southeast.

Perhaps because of a breakdown in the handover from the towers
to departures, it had caught the controller unaware, or with insufficient time to resolve the developing conflict with us. To this, add a
wrong call. Our original track would have made us a fast-moving
target from right to left, but our steep left turn had suspended us in
space directly in its path.

End of story? Not quite! The flight continued and all normal
operations were resumed? Well yes, to a point. Logical thinking can
become corrosive after such a fright and for me the question 'what
did we do wrong?' would not go away.

I wasn't prepared for the coming emotional confusion, jangled
nerves and eroding confidence and certainty. For the remainder of

this flight and for many months to come I was distrustful of everything aviation, reviewing actions constantly, looking for the hidden danger in checklists and communications and having to psych myself to overcome the uncertainty that pervaded my brain.

In quiet moments, even some thirty years later, the mind endlessly plays a closed loop scenario with a different outcome. As a company policy all cockpit communications were conducted via the headset at all times, and all aircraft had a hot microphone system. I'm convinced I would have missed the controller's heads-up, if we had been on cockpit speaker. But then again ... if I had been less responsive in initiating the turn we would have sailed through blissfully unaware.

NOTES:

POOR PASSENGER BEHAVIOUR

CHIRP

Nov 2016, Issue 120

I have reported the increasing frequency of shockingly bad passenger behaviour many times over the years. It is getting worse and worse each season. The frequency and predictability is also getting worse. There is an obvious and clear endemic issue with bad, and criminal behaviour on UK flights.

In addition to the routes note for poor passenger behaviour over many years, there are now issues on many other routes i.e. the problem is becoming more and more common and widespread. This season it has been made known to me that [ ]-based crew have recently been: attacked and held by the throat, thrown against the a/c galley; a sexual assault.

These incidents are predictable and largely preventable. We see the behaviour, we know the flights likely to be affected; the local police know this; the airline knows this. It is NOT being prevented. It is highly likely there will be a serious physical assault which will cause serious injury / hospitalisation / the ending of staff members' careers.

As a secondary point, our low cost flights are bringing the industry into serious disrepute. I feel so very sorry for the innocent, well behaved families, older passengers, children who have to sit near these yobs, and listen to vile, offensive language for 3 hours.

In my opinion, it is the biggest preventable safety risk we now face as pilots in the UK.

Lessons Learned:

Protect your crew as much as is possible. Press for prosecutions.

CHIRP Comment: Members of the CHIRP Cabin Crew and Air Transport Advisory Boards have confirmed the severity and frequency of the problems reported above. Much of the bad behaviour appears to be alcohol-fuelled, although other substances, including illegal drugs, are likely to be involved. The availability of alcohol at airports is a difficult issue because of the revenue generated by sales and there is inconsistency among airlines about preventing drunken passengers from boarding; some operators ask handling agents to turn away passengers considered to be intoxicated while others require handling agents to contact the flight crew. The removal of passengers from aircraft by the police is not uncommon in the UK but in some countries the police may be less cooperative and/or national procedures may be more restrictive. However, more could be done to warn passengers about poor behaviour at the point of ticket sale; this would enable warnings to be targeted at those routes and airports known to be problematic.

Cabin crew and innocent passengers should not be required to put up with boorish behaviour, bad or sexist language, let alone the more extreme behaviour reported above. Nor should the safety implications of such behaviour be overlooked, including the distraction for flight crew and the dilemma of deciding whether to divert the aircraft. Miscreants should be prosecuted notwithstanding that it could take a year or more for cases to reach court and require crew members to give evidence. Supporting evidence is vital for a successful prosecution. Identifying the individuals involved and making notes about the incident as soon as possible can be helpful; if possible, identify other passengers who might be prepared to give evidence. Short of prosecution, "difficulty in controlling intoxicated, violent or unruly passengers" is a mandatory reportable occurrence under EU law. Conscientious reporting is essential and operators should encourage flight crew and cabin crew to report every instance of poor behaviour.

Poor passenger behaviour creates an intolerable working environment for the cabin crew, undermines the authority of the entire crew and affects the safety of everyone on board. The Authority and Industry are aware of the problem and it has been raised in the media recently. Nevertheless, CHIRP intends to draw this Report and the views of its Cabin Crew and Air Transport Advisory Boards to the CAA Av Sec and to the (UK industry) Flight Operations Liaison Group 'for information', stating that CHIRP fully supports industry action that is being taken.

NOTES:

CHAPTER 5

WEATHER, WIND & ICE

"Just remember, if you crash because of weather, your funeral will be held on a sunny day."
Layton A. Bennett

THE DE-ICING COMMUNICATIONS
VACUUM - A321

CALLBACK

Nov 2016, Issue 442

[We were] dispatched with an inoperative APU due to APU inlet icing while operating in freezing rain. [We] proceeded to the de-ice pad and contacted Snowman on the assigned frequency. [We explained] our APU problem and notified them four to six times that we had both engines running.... [We were] informed, as we entered [the de-ice] pad, to shut down the number 1 engine for de-ice and anti-ice fluid application. As we [set] the parking brakes and prepared to shut down the engine, Snowman informed us that de-ice personnel had approached the aircraft too soon and had [a] headset sucked into the number 1 engine. After ensuring [that the] employee was safe and unharmed, we contacted ATC, Operations, Maintenance, and Ramp, and returned to the gate.

NOTES:

SPECIFICATIONS MORE LIKE GUIDELINES

CALLBACK

Nov 2016, Issue 442

[We] requested de-ice and anti-ice fluid treatment after pushback.... Station personnel sprayed the aircraft with Type I and Type IV fluids.... After being sprayed and commencing taxi to the runway, ATC advised us of a ground stop to our destination, so we returned to the gate. While sitting at the gate for some time, the First Officer and I both noticed snow accumulating on top of both wings after only approximately 45 minutes since the commencement of the application of the Type IV fluid. We pointed out the snow accumulation to the station personnel...to make sure that they understood that the Type IV fluid was not holding up to the minimum holdover time. After our release by ATC, we had the aircraft de-iced and anti-iced again in the same manner and departed without delay to our destination.

The First Officer and I both reviewed the holdover tables for the Clariant fluid, making sure that we were looking at the proper table and reading it correctly. I don't know why the Type IV fluid under-performed its holdover time.

NOTES:

MISSED TRIM AND MIS-TRIMMED - B737

CALLBACK

Nov 2016, Issue 442

[The] first push was on time. A significant delay occurred waiting for [our] first de-ice attempt.... A cabin check was made, and frozen precipitation was observed on the cabin side of both engine nacelles. ... We were deiced a second time. We did another cabin check, but the aircraft still had frozen precipitation in the same locations. Because of the extended ground time, we taxied back to the gate.... We spoke with the Supervisor at the gate, [who]... said that an experienced crew would do the [next] de-icing procedure. They also requested that we trim the aircraft full nose down...to de-ice. As our procedure calls to de-ice in the green band, we had the [trim] as far forward as possible, but remaining in the green [band]. This did result in having to note the trim setting not being [set to] the proper [value] in the Before Push Checklist. We...mentioned the need to reset the trim after de-icing. This time, we decided to do a cabin check at the point of de-icing.... Once again, we did not have a clean aircraft. Another call was made to Ops to de-ice again. Engines were shut down and we again described the location of the snow and contamination.... This fourth and final de-ice procedure was conducted with radio communication directly with the de-ice truck. They did a double check of each problem area and stated that they could see there was no contamination. The Captain did a cabin check and confirmed [that we now had] a clean aircraft.

Post de-icing checklists were done, and we were finally at [the runway].... We were cleared by Tower for takeoff and I taxied slowly onto the runway due to the ice and snow present and fair braking reports by other aircraft. After lining up and confirming the runway, I gave control of the thrust levers to the First Officer. As he advanced the thrust levers, we got a takeoff warning horn. I took control of the aircraft and quickly determined...that the trim, although it looked in the front edge of the green, was clearly not at the [correct] takeoff setting and was the source of the horn. We told Tower we needed to clear the runway.

NOTES:

BETTER LATE THAN NEVER - B737

CALLBACK

Nov 2016, Issue 442

This B737 Captain was distracted with his wing anti-ice configuration during takeoff. The result was unintentional, but a significant deviation to the takeoff procedure occurred.

From the Captain's report:

[It was a] flaps 1 takeoff on compacted snow. [I] began the takeoff roll with engine heat and wing anti-ice on. After the "V1" call, [I] became distracted by the [wing] anti-ice configuration, causing [me] to miss the..."Rotate" call. [I] rotated approximately 35 to 40 knots late.

From the First Officer's report:

The Captain became distracted by the [wing] anti-ice on configuration right at the point I was making the "Rotate" call, requesting that I turn the wing anti-ice off. (The Wing Anti-Ice Switch was in the ON position with the blue valve position lights illuminated, indicating [the valves] had closed as designed.) I repeated the "Rotate" call two more times in quick succession, and the [Captain] rotated late.

NOTES:

SLIDING INTO HOME - A320

CALLBACK

Nov 2016, Issue 442

[As we approached] the gate, there were no personnel to guide us in. The taxi-in line was covered in snow. After a few minutes, rampers appeared in tugs and on foot. The ramp was slippery as indicated by a ramper falling down.... The tugs were sliding as well. We waited a few more minutes to be marshalled in. Finally the marshallers showed up, and we proceeded into the gate indicating 1 knot on the ground speed readout. I was purposely very cautious on the taxi in. We were given the [normal] stop signal, and [I] set the brakes. The aircraft continued to slide forward even though the brakes were set. The residual thrust at idle was enough to move the aircraft on the ramp under these conditions. The aircraft was not going to hit anything or anyone, but I was helpless at this point. I indicated to the marshaller to get the chocks in. He didn't have any!!! I turned on the yellow pump and decided to shut down the engines in hopes [that] the loss of the residual thrust would help. It did. The aircraft stopped sliding. What a helpless feeling.... We were lucky that nothing was touched or damaged. Fortunately the jetway was very far away from its normal position.

NOTES:

AIRCRAFT DEPARTING WITH CONTAMINATED WING

CHIRP

Feb 2017, Issue 121

I was a passenger, but Professional licence holder on flight [ ] on [ ] Dec 2016. I was standing at the gate and watched the turnaround before boarding [the aircraft]. During the turnaround I did not personally witness anyone conduct a tactile inspection of the upper wing surface.

Upon boarding, I noticed the upper wing surface appeared to have frost on it which was growing from the outer 2/3 of the wing to the tip including the spoiler panels and aileron. The apron was well lit with flood lights. The METAR at the time was [ ] 2020Z 24003KT CAVOK M03/M03 Q1027 NOSIG.

I was becoming concerned that no de-icing would take place. As we prepared to push back I got up from my seat and went to the rear galley to ask the cabin crew if we were going to de-ice. The crew at the rear galley contacted the front who spoke to the pilot to raise my concerns who said he was happy to depart. I persisted and told the crew I would not sit down until an inspection had taken place.

The Commander came and glanced out of the windows and then

came to see me. I told him I believed there to be frost on the wing at which point he asked me if I knew the fuel temperature and walked off. I was taken aback, as I agree the fuel could melt the frost. However, it only appeared after the landing and I believe the dew in the air would freeze. I am not convinced fuel can de frost cold soaked ailerons and spoiler panels that are NOT in direct contact with the wing that has fuel in it.

The aircraft departed and there were no consequences. Personally I should have refused to depart on the aircraft until either a tactile check had been conducted or de-icing taken place considering the temp Mo3/Mo3.

The problem as you can see from pictures I can provide [pictures not included in FEEDBACK] is either of us could have been correct. The ONLY way to check would have been a tactile inspection with a temp of Mo3/Mo3. I do not believe that the Commander could have been certain he departed with a clean wing without a tactile inspection, even if the fuel temperature was above Zero given the conditions and the view of the wing.

Lessons Learned:

In the future, travelling as a passenger I would not have sat down and would have stood my ground until a tactile inspection would have taken place.

CHIRP Comment: On receipt of the CHIRP report the operator asked the operating aircraft Commander to file an ASR before conducting an incident review. The investigation accepted that the Commander had carried out a pre-flight inspection and at that time the wings were clear of contamination. The Commander did not knowingly dispatch with contaminated wings but realises now that he should have given more consideration to the passenger's concerns at the time.

Advice from passengers is a difficult area. There are well-documented cases where passengers have alerted crews to problems that might otherwise have gone unnoticed. However, well-intentioned advice from unqualified passengers can be a huge distraction. If there is an opportunity to do so, establishing the credibility of the passenger might help in applying "due consideration" to strike the appropriate balance.

Pilots are used to dealing with anti-icing and de-icing issues. Some aircraft types are particularly sensitive to very light frost and others are permitted to allow frost in localised areas; fuel temperature is a relevant factor, another being whether the wing is metal or composite. All these factors could cause confusion in a passenger's mind about the true status of a 'clean wing' and failing to reassure nervous passengers could lead to a disruptive passenger incident. Caution should be the over-riding watchword.

NOTES:

WHAT DID THESE CAPTAINS REALLY MEAN?

CALLBACK

Aug 2017, Issue 451

The Providence Field Condition (FICON) was 5/5/5 with thin snow, and ATIS was [reporting] 1/2 mile visibility with snow. The braking report from [the] previous B757 was good. Upon breaking out of the clouds, we saw an all-white runway with areas that looked as if they had previously been plowed in the centre, but were now covered with snow. Landing occurred with auto-brakes 3, but during rollout I overrode the brakes by gently pressing harder. However, no matter how hard I pressed on the brakes, the aircraft only gradually slowed down. Tower asked me if I could expedite to the end.... I said, "NO," as the runway felt pretty slick to me. I reported medium braking both to the Tower and via ACARS to Dispatch. A follow-on light corporate commuter aircraft reported good braking.

I was a member of the Takeoff And Landing Performance Assessment (TALPA) advisory group...and am intimately familiar with braking action physics as well as the Runway Condition Assessment Matrix (RCAM). There was no way the braking was good or the snow was 1/8th inch or less in depth.

I would [suggest that] data...be collected from the aircraft...to analyze the aircraft braking coefficient.... It would also be of value to ascertain the delivered brake pressure versus the commanded pressure for this event, as there can sometimes be a large disparity in friction-limited landings. I think that pilots do not really know how to give braking action reports, and I don't think the airport wanted to take my report of medium braking seriously. I also think pilots need to know how to use the RCAM to evaluate probable runway conditions that may differ from the FICON. Additionally, there is no such description as "thin" in the RCAM. None of the FAA Advisory Circulars that include the RCAM have thin snow as part of depth description.

NOTES:

DON'T WAIT TO DISSEMINATE; AUTOMATE

CALLBACK

A Phoenix Tower Controller experienced and identified a common problem while disseminating an URGENT PIREP. He offers a potential solution, technique, and rationale.

While working Clearance Delivery, I received an URGENT PIREP via Flight Data Input/Output General Information (FDIO GI) message stating, "URGENT PIREP...DRO [location] XA30Z [time] 140 [altitude] BE40 [type] SEV RIME ICING...." This was especially important to me to have this information since we have several flights daily going to Durango, Colorado. My technique would be to not only make a blanket transmission about the PIREP, but also specifically address flights going to that location to advise them and make sure they received the information. The issue is that...I did not receive this URGENT PIREP until [1:20 after it had been reported]. Severe icing can cause an aircraft incident or accident in a matter of moments. It is unacceptable that it takes one hour and twenty minutes to disseminate this information.

[A] better PIREP sharing system [is needed.] PIREPs should be entered in AISR [Aeronautical Information System Replacement] immediately after receiving the report and should automatically be disseminated to facilities within a specified radius without having to be manually entered again by a Traffic Management Unit or Weather Contractor, etc.

NOTES:

INFORMING THE INTELLIGENT DECISION - C402

CALLBACK

During my descent I was assigned 6,000 feet by Approach... I entered a layer of clouds about 8,000 feet. I turned on the aircraft's anti-icing equipment. I levelled at 6,000 feet and noticed the propeller anti-ice [ammeter] was indicating that the equipment was not operational. I looked at the circuit breaker and saw that the right one was popped.

I informed ATC of my equipment failure. Approach requested and received a PIREP from traffic ahead of me indicating that there was ice in the clouds, but the bases were about 5,500 to 5,000 feet. Some light mixed ice was developing on my airframe. My experience [with] the ice that day was mostly light [with] some pockets of moderate around 5,000 to 6,000 feet. I informed [Dispatch] of my situation and elected to continue to [my destination] as I was close to the bottom of the icing layer, and a climb through it to divert would have prolonged exposure to the ice.

NOTES:

IF THE CONTROLLER'S AWAY, THE PILOTS CAN STRAY

CALLBACK

Aug 2017, Issue 451

I was working alone in the tower cab, all combined Tower and Approach positions, at the beginning of a mid-shift. Weather had been moving through the area with gusty winds and precipitation in the area.... Aircraft X checked [in while] descending via the SADYL [arrival] and immediately reported moderate turbulence.

I issued a clearance to... JIMMI as a vector for sequencing with a descent to 9,000 feet. The instruction was read back correctly, and I observed Aircraft X turn left toward the fix and continue descending. I obtained some additional information from Aircraft X concerning the turbulence. At that point I went to the computer in the back of the room and logged on to the AISR website to enter a PIREP for the moderate turbulence. After successfully [completing that task,] ... I walked back to the radar scope and observed Aircraft X descending through 8,000 feet. I instructed them to climb to 9,000 feet. The Pilot replied that they were descending to 6,000 feet. I again instructed them to climb to 9,000 feet and informed them that they were in a 9,000 foot Minimum Vectoring Altitude (MVA) area. They began climbing and reached approximately 8,400 feet before they crossed into a 7,000 foot MVA [area.] The 6,000 foot altitude is the final altitude on the arrival, and I suspect they missed entering the new altitude into the FMS.

The responsibility to enter the PIREP into AISR instead of transmitting it verbally to FSS resulted in my being away from the radar scope as the aircraft descended through their assigned altitude.... [We should] return the responsibility of computer based PIREP entry to FSS to allow Controllers to focus on the operation.

NOTES:

THE EFFECTIVE PARTY-LINE PIREP - B787

CALLBACK

Aug 2017, Issue 451

The [aural] warning... sounded like the autopilot disconnect button. We immediately looked at the instruments and noticed that the airspeed was in the red zone and our altitude was off by -500 feet. The Captain reduced the throttles, but airspeed continued to increase, so [he] opened the speed brakes slightly. I noticed that yellow slash bars were indicated on both LNAV and VNAV. I told the Captain, "No LNAV or VNAV, engines look fine." The Captain disconnected the autopilot while continuing to get the airspeed under control and regain our altitude back to FL380. I reset the flight directors, selected Heading Select, and set V/S to +300. I reengaged LNAV/VNAV and informed the Captain that these systems were available...

We were both stunned as to what had happened because the ride was smooth and had no bumps or chop at all. I immediately got on the radio and told another aircraft behind us (one that we had been communicating with and passing PIREP information) that we had just experienced something very erratic and strange. As I was making this call, a printer message came across the printer about a B777 that had experienced severe wave turbulence at FL350 in the same vicinity as [our encounter.] I relayed this information to the aircraft behind us. They informed us that, yes, they had just encountered the same and gained 1,000 feet and 50 knots. There were other aircraft in the area who later confirmed that they experienced the same wave, however were better prepared to handle it due to our detailed PIREPs, and [those crews] were very appreciative.

We sent a message to Dispatch. Dispatch did not show any unusual activity such as horizontal windshear or unusual jet streams in the area and was...surprised to get our [PIREP].

NOTES:

TEASING A TORONTO TAILWIND - A319

CALLBACK

July 2017, Issue 450

After being delayed due to low ceilings in Toronto, we were finally descending...in heavy rain and moderate turbulence with clearance to 7,000 feet MSL. After a third 360 degree turn, we were...transferred to the Final Controller and proceeded inbound for the ILS RWY 05. The last several ATIS [reports] showed winds at approximately 090 to 100 [degrees] at 5 to 10 knots, and the Final Controller mentioned the same with an RVR of 6,000 plus feet for Runway 05. When cleared for the approach, we were at 3,000 feet MSL to intercept the glideslope, and I noticed the winds had picked up to a 50 knot direct tailwind. The First Officer was flying. We were assigned 160 knots and began to configure at approximately 2,000 feet AGL. At 1,500 feet the wind was a 30 knot direct tailwind and we had flaps 3. Indicated airspeed (IAS) had increased at this point [with] thrust at idle to 170-175 knots, prohibiting final flaps just yet. The First Officer did a great job aggressively trying to slow the aircraft, as we were concerned about getting a flaps 3 overspeed. As I knew from the ATIS and the Controllers (Tower now), the winds were to die off very soon to less than 10 knots. [Below] 1,000 feet we were just getting the airspeed to put in final flaps (full) and were finally stabilized and on speed between 500 to 800 feet. The winds were now at the reported 090 [degrees] at 8 knots or so [below] 500 feet. The total wind shift was approximately 90 degrees from direct tailwind to a right crosswind - losing 40 knots [of tailwind] in the space of 1,500 feet or so. The reasons I elected to continue the approach were:

1. [I knew] about the wind shift and decrease [in tailwind] as reported on the ATIS and from ATC.
2. [I saw] a positive trend in the wind.
3. [I was] prepared for the missed approach (at 500 feet) IF the winds and IAS stayed as they were earlier in the approach. We landed uneventfully in the touchdown zone and on speed...after breaking out before minimums.

Comment:

Windshear has existed for as long as aviators have taken to the skies and is largely responsible for several classic aviation losses. Notable U.S. aviation accidents include Eastern Flight 66 (1975), Pan American Flight 759 (1982), and Delta Flight 191 (1985).

Windshear remained unrecognized for years. It was not clearly understood until swept wing, jet aircraft encountered the phenomenon. Since 1975, windshear has been researched and studied, measured, defined, catalogued, and rightly vilified. Technology has been developed to identify and minimize the threats that it poses. Procedures have been implemented to aid pilots who experience windshear in flight and flight crews invest hours of simulator training practicing windshear escape manoeuvres.

Even with progress to date, windshear continues to be a worthy adversary to aviation professionals. It requires respect and wisdom to defeat. Pilots often must make decisions regarding known or anticipated windshear, and the best practice is always avoidance.

NOTES:

UP AND DOWN INTO SALT LAKE CITY

CALLBACK

July 2017, Issue 450

We had lined up for the ILS RWY 3 at Ogden, but at glideslope intercept, the weather had [deteriorated] to ¼ mile visibility and a 400 foot ceiling. We broke off the approach,...requested an approach to land at Salt Lake City, and were vectored to the ILS RWY 34L. Approximately 10 miles downwind in solid IMC [with the] autopilot and altitude hold on and about to turn base, we hit a downdraft that dropped us approximately 2,000 feet. The horizon ball was all brown, the autopilot and altitude [hold function] were ineffective, the loss of control set off the master warning system due to lack of fuel (at the time we had 750 pounds per side), and the terrain warning went off. Recovery was accomplished, but with a 2,000 foot gain (assigned altitude [had been] 10,000 feet; at the floor of the incident [the altitude was] approximately 8,000 feet; at the ceiling of incident [the altitude was] approximately 12,000 feet). I was then routed back to the west and north on vectors for sequencing back to the ILS RWY 34L at Salt Lake City that was shot with a side-step on final in VFR conditions to RWY 34R.

NOTES:

SHEARING SITUATIONAL AWARENESS

CALLBACK

July 2017, Issue 450

We were on final for Runway 8R in Houston and encountered wind-shear.... Tower started calling an approach wind loss of 20 knots that increased to 25 knots at a 3 mile final. The Copilot and I were discussing what constituted a microburst alert, which was 30 knots, so we elected to continue the approach. We were in moderate turbulence and the wind was currently a right quartering tailwind which would switch to a left crosswind on the runway. I asked the Copilot to increase our target speed to plus 20, which he did, and as we approached the outer marker, we were fully configured and on speed. At approximately 1,400 feet AGL, we received a "MONITOR RADAR DISPLAY." I saw that the indication was ahead of us to the right of our course. Since we were still stable and fully configured [with the] autopilot and auto-throttles on, we elected to continue.

Shortly we received the call, "GO AROUND, WINDSHEAR AHEAD." I initiated the go-around and asked for flaps 15 and gear up. Very shortly after this, we received the call, "WINDSHEAR, WINDSHEAR, WINDSHEAR." At that point I pushed the throttles to the stops, verified the spoilers were stowed, and selected Takeoff Go-Around (TOGA) again. The First Officer called ATC and said we were going around. I was so focused on flying the plane with regards to Radio Altimeter (RA) and trend, and verifying I was doing everything correctly, I did not hear what ATC replied back to us. Adding to the workload and task saturation was the plane on Runway 8L, which also went around, and then the two planes behind us on Runways 8L and 8R also went around.

The Copilot advised that ATC said to level off at 2,000 feet as we were passing through 2,000 feet with a high climb rate. I still had "WINDSHEAR" displayed on my ADI, and I told him I was not going to level off. He then had to try to talk to ATC again to get a new altitude. They gave us 3,000 feet. We were climbing rapidly, and I brought the throttles back to level off at 3,000 feet, but overshot it to approximately 3,200 feet and descended back to 3,000 feet. The landing gear horn immediately began to sound when I pulled the power back since we still had flaps 15. I made sure we were above flaps 15 retraction speed, and we completed a normal go-around at that point to clean manoeuvring speed.

Everything happened so fast. ATC should not give a level off altitude of 2,000 feet since I now know it is possible to still be in windshear...at that altitude. If I were to fly this approach again, I would elect to abort the approach and wait for tower to stop calling a 20-25 knot loss at a 3 mile final.... We thought that since the planes ahead of us were landing, we would be able to [as well]. Obviously there is always a first flight that cannot land, and on this day, that was us.

NOTES:

THE FINAL AUTHORITY — 14 CFR 91.3

CALLBACK

July 2017, Issue 450

This heavy transport Captain perceived a subtle suggestion to take off when weather that may have presented a windshear hazard was nearby. He exercised his authority with seasoned wisdom and sound judgment when he opted not to leverage the safety of his aircraft or crew.

As we were taxiing west on Runway 27, we could see a radar return of a strong storm which was depicted red on our screen. The storm was directly west of the...airport and appeared to be moving east toward us. As we turned south on Taxiway N, we could only see part of the storm to our right on the radar display. When we switched frequencies to Tower, we heard that there was windshear on a two mile final for our runway. As we approached the runway, we advised Tower that we would not take off. Tower reminded us that the windshear was two miles in the opposite direction from where we would be heading. It seemed like the cell was directly over the field at that time, possibly centered a little north.... The FOM guides us not to get within 5 miles of a cell below FL200. Tower instructed us to taxi out of the way so that several other aircraft could take off while we waited a few minutes for the storm to pass.

I feel that Tower was more concerned about getting airplanes on their way than waiting a few minutes until it was safe. I also think [there is an] air carrier culture pressure to get the job done even if there is an increased risk.

When one aircraft decides it is not safe to take off, perhaps Tower should inform the following aircraft that might not have been on frequency to get the same information. Although several aircraft took off away from the storm, they faced the possibility of getting a decreasing performance windshear on takeoff.

NOTES:

MOUNTAIN MADNESS

CASA

Name withheld by request, Mar 28, 2014

We were sitting absolutely still on the runway when it began to rain. The captain was crying and I wanted to throw up.

A few hours earlier I had been enjoying a perfect Anzac Day poolside in Cairns. I was on reserve as a regional airline first officer, but as we had no scheduled flights on public holidays, I was certain my standby status was simply a formality. Then the phone rang: a charter to Tabubil in Papua New Guinea taking mine workers from Cairns, as their regular aircraft had become unserviceable.

I was inexperienced in PNG operations, and felt somewhat apprehensive. I knew Tabubil was a short, one-way, gravel runway embedded in the beginning of a valley with a 12,000-foot mountain range in very close proximity. Tabubil is set in extremely dense jungle fed by one of the highest rainfalls in the world. No wonder it has such a poor history of aircraft safety – almost 50 lives lost in two decades.

From the pre-departure weather forecast, we knew there would be passing showers and only one possible direction for landing, which would see us conduct a straight-in GPS-RNAV or 'cloud-break procedure' (in PNG CAA terms).

We began our descent, flying over what we deemed our alternate aerodrome. The town of Kiunga 30nm to the south was CAVOK, with flat terrain, but we knew, if we diverted there, that only drum Jet A-1 was available, and over-wing refuelling of our turboprop was no easy feat.

With the cabin secure, the aircraft fully configured and the captain flying, I advanced the propeller levers to full fine, my duty at the final approach fix. Looking outside, we were in VMC but on top of a thick layer of stratus cloud. I was unsure if we'd even enter cloud before the minimum descent altitude. We reached the MDA and then the missed approach point without even entering cloud.

We could see nothing of the aerodrome. The go-around was uneventful. At a safe altitude, we discussed our options. We had plenty of fuel and Kiunga was available. We also discussed a second approach, as we knew the showers were moving through fast.

We flew another missed approach and were again manoeuvring safely on top of cloud visually. The 12,000-feet monster at the end of the valley was shiny to look at as it popped out of the cloud. After the prior discussion with the captain I was comfortable that we'd then divert to Kiunga. Instead he asked my opinion on manoeuvring visually, north of our position to the south of the mountain range, to 'get a closer look down the valley through the passing showers'.

I immediately felt uncomfortable. Two missed approaches are enough in my opinion. Moreover, while on the missed approach, I had heard a Twin Otter taxi, backtrack and line up on the reciprocal runway. Manoeuvring further north we could see passing gaps in the fast-moving stratus, with occasional glimpses of the six lead-in strobes in the valley. What occurred next left me frozen in shock. The captain disconnected the autopilot and immediately put our turbo-prop in a steep descent through a gap while yelling 'I'm visual!'

I could not believe what was happening. I felt betrayed and cheated. We'd agreed a plan of action and this moment of impulsiveness had intervened. The tension in the flight deck increased instantly. The captain loudly called for full flap and landing gear down while he pushed the plane into a steep descent. Having been a skydive pilot, I thought my days of steep, rushed descents were behind me. I then had a horrifying realisation: the Twin Otter! I yelled at the captain: 'there's a Twin Otter taking off and we've told him we're on a missed approach!'

The captain was in a state of tunnel vision. He yelled at me to 'tell them to get off the runway, we're landing!' Five minutes of sheer terror had begun. 'TRAFFIC TRAFFIC!' then 'CLIMB CLIMB, TCAS CLIMB' screamed our onboard Traffic Collision Advisory System. I could see the target on my TCAS indicator climbing and coming straight at us. 'This cannot be happening' I remember thinking. 'TCAS wants us to climb, we have thick cloud above us; we are visual now, committed to this narrow valley where the chart says circling prohibited!'

The captain reduced the descent rate and we became visual with the Twin Otter. It was close. Very close. I will never forget the look on its pilot's face. Our steep profile was interrupted, and now couldn't possibly land straight in. We were committed to the valley, there was no plan B. I've never been without a 'plan B'! We were visual but there were walls of stratus cloud everywhere I looked. And, I knew with certainty, large rock walls looming just behind the clouds. The captain levelled out and began screaming over and over again, 'I'm visual'. Overhead the aerodrome, he put our turboprop into a 60-degree left-hand turn. The Enhanced Ground Proximity Warning System (EGPWS) sounded its first of many warnings. 'BANK ANGLE! BANK ANGLE!'. Out of my window I could see nothing but cloud. I thought we'd entered it.

In desperation, I did the only thing I could think of. I turned the weather radar to terrain mode, fed directly from the EGPWS's onboard GPS. There was close terrain, with glimpses of yellow and red (terrain above).

Things turned quiet for a moment. We'd returned to wings levels on a close, pseudo downwind when the captain began another steep descent. The flight had become single-pilot ops by this stage. We were now visual, although very high. Another acute left-hand turn and the EGPWS came to life once more. BANK ANGLE! BANK ANGLE!, followed by SINK RATE! SINK RATE! We turned final, with an extremely high descent rate. I remember screaming 'we are way too high!'

Intonations of SINK RATE! SINK RATE! PULL UP! PULL UP! accompanied our very short final. At a few hundred feet we were back, momentarily, on a normal profile. The captain reduced the rate of descent and flared the aircraft and we touched down very hard, followed by a bounce. Another bounce, then full reverse thrust, and our aircraft showed off its short field capabilities.

We were sitting absolutely still on the runway when it began to rain. I didn't want to say anything. The rain was pelting down, like a theatre curtain after a command performance. I had begun my after-landing scan when the captain asked me to 'say something!' I sat in silence as I mustered the courage to look at him. He was crying. I said nothing. We taxied to the terminal in silence. A chime from the intercom: the flight attendant said the passengers wanted to congratulate us on getting them on the ground safely. I felt sick to my core – all I wanted to do was throw up.

The passengers disembarked and the captain disappeared to the terminal for an hour. The flight attendant was really shaken. She later told me she'd been rehearsing her impact drill and commands as she thought – correctly – that we were in serious trouble.

We were lucky that day. No mission is worth those sorts of risks.

Yes, over-wing refuelling post diversion would have been a headache, but not nearly as big a headache as flying into a mountainside. Crew resource management can swing in an instant, so always be on the lookout!

NOTES:

HOW WAS YOUR JOURNEY?

CASA

Mar 25, 2014

British-based airline pilot Mark Mannering-Smith evokes how quickly a flight can turn from sightseeing to intense planning. And the best part? None of the passengers suspected a thing...

The idle chatter has died down. Since leaving the ocean we have been sliding over the vast and limitless beauty of Canada's Atlantic coast. It's rare to get such a consistently clear view all the way from the cracking sea ice right down to the blossoming fringes of Boston. Patches of civilisation spur speculation about the communities below. The thrust levers rock gently under my right hand, responding to the ripples of instability in the upper atmosphere. The tops of the levers are worn smooth by years of use, but the gentle roar of the RBs, (Rolls-Royce RB211 turbofans), puffing and blowing of the air-conditioning systems, and whine of the chiller units just behind the flight deck, combine to make a faithful and familiar thrum. Everything is just fine.

I scan the instrumentation. As we cross another waypoint, LNAV (lateral navigation) imperceptibly adjusts to make good the next one. Hundreds of miles of electronic breadcrumbs stretch out far ahead and into the United States. Down to the left Stephenville sits bleakly in the jaws of a broad inlet on the west coast of Newfoundland. Normally just a circle on a chart, Stephenville cuts a surprisingly meek stance, with houses fringing the inlet before petering out—civilisation giving way to the wilderness once more. The chart-based brother of Stephenville is far bolder: good approaches, long runways, excellent facilities capable of hosting 180 tonnes of airliner. It doesn't mention the pretty spit of land positioned shyly across the water. You'd miss all the good stuff diverting there in the darkness or in the gloom of a Canadian winter.

The ACARS (aircraft communications addressing and reporting system) is back up and running and a little burst of weather requests has brought the printer to life. Strings of coded data give us wind, visibility, precipitation, cloud, temperature, pressure. The familiar argot tells us a surprising story: wind, rain and storms are thrashing Dulles. A flicker of recognition passes between us. Back in London, six hours ago, we had both seen the thin arc of forecast convective weather stretching from New York to DC. Not a single airport had thought it significant enough to include in their forecast. I could maybe forgive them for missing the full brimstone treatment in their predictions, but I'd have thought that the combined forecasting brains and computers of the entire East Coast might have been slightly more accurate than the 'clear skies and light winds' song played in the earlier forecasts.

There's no space for chatter now. We are busy hoovering up information to help us make some decisions. We are really looking for some staging points on which to build a plan. The sky is breaking up, with the ragged edges of unstable air beginning to surround us. I'm moving the radar up and down looking for clues about the depth and extent of the weather. The controllers are great—Dulles has been shut for a while. Looks like it is open again, but heavy weather is between us.

I give the aircraft to Ed so I can talk to our cabin crew. We come up with a strategy to speed the last of the service along. Everyone is aware that there may be some bumps. They also know that we are going to be a little busy looking for some smooth, clean air. Back facing the front it's obvious that we need to route around some weather. We've identified some points of the route where we are going to review fuel and time. The weather radar isn't great at seeing around corners: bigger storms can hide whole systems in their shadow, so what looks like a good route can sometimes close up or change on the far side.

Back in the mid levels now. Tops tower above us and little crackles of electrical activity break through on the radio. Pop. Dark pools of shade sidle up to us. We've a high- and low-fuel figure for a couple of places between us and Dulles where we can make an objective assessment of how things are going and whether we might need to exercise our insurance policies.

Philadelphia and Atlantic City are both clear and look like useful boltholes should Dulles shut again. I ask Ed to turn the fuel figures into a time. Two reasons: I want him to check my maths, and I want to remove any subjectivity from the numbers on the gauges. Any diversion is busy—even if it is half-planned already—so if we go somewhere I want to punch the stopwatch so that we have a clean and visual count up to our endurance limit.

So we've a strategy with some good contingency to cover several different options. A long and frequently elastic RNAV (area navigation) arrival is another variable: New York have limited information on our routing, but Potomac are on the ball. As Ed teases us around towering cumulus, we negotiate some airspace. We are back on the speed—no sense rushing—and there's a gentle beauty to the unfolding clouds. 'Pretty, that.'

This little gap is perfectly smooth. The kind of air that's thick and wet with recent storm but has lost all compunction to jostle you around.

More scanning of the radar. I offer Ed a range of headings just in case. We've an eye on mileage. Very simple maths running in another part of our brains keeps us on top of whether we can make the airport without any further drama. The brooding clouds seem to be leaving us with another little joke. Our fear of extended routings and diversions could be replaced by a routing straight to final approach, perhaps leaving us with a straight energy issue. Cabin is all done now. They're a great little team and they know the score.

Gap controller is interested in whether we can route to finals. No problem. Ed has done a perfect job of trading height, speed, and energy. A few jolts on the back side of another CU. We are about 15 miles out now. A sprawling mass of rain is skirting the far side of the field. It's painting heavily on the radar but it simply doesn't feel as if there's any energy left. We switch early to tower who tell us that the surface wind is just two knots. Really? Apparently we missed the real fun over the past hour.

The runway is wet but well drained. We review braking and go-around options. Right turns do not look like much of an option, regardless of my hunch about it being all rained out. Smooth all the way in. Nice touchdown. I'll take that one, thank you.

Fat raindrops beat on the windshield as we taxi in. It's difficult to decide what's worse; peering through the thick rivulets, or listening to the howl of the wiper system. SAS take ages to clear our gate. I spend a few moments thinking about how we had to continually flex our strategy, only to arrive in Washington and just kind of land.

It almost seemed a bit unfinished, with the lack of any drama at all. Is that maybe the game?

NOTES:

POWER PLUS ATTITUDE - FALCON 900

CASA

May 20, 2016

Night over the Pacific. A Falcon 900 returning to Perth from the United States via Honolulu and Townsville.

The aircraft was operated by three pilots acting in rotation, and on the sector from Honolulu to Townsville I was the resting pilot. A flight attendant was also part of the crew.

The only passenger was the company chief executive.

Several hours into the flight, with the aircraft cruising in smooth air, the chief executive and I were both asleep in the cabin when I was aroused by a short series of sharp vibrations similar to the tugging of a fish on a line. Moderate intensity. It stopped as suddenly as it started.

I sat up and the chief executive said to me in an agitated voice: 'Hey Max, what the ##### was that?'

I said, 'I don't know,' because I didn't know. 'But I'll go and find out.'

As I spoke, there was another short set of vibrations. Then, within a second or two of my leaving the seat the aircraft bunted very positively and I hit my head on the ceiling. A couple more bounces off the ceiling and I reached the cockpit door.

This was no longer a polite enquiry. Alarmed now I said to the captain: 'What the hell is going on?' or words to that effect.

His reply: 'The aeroplane's stalling and we've got to get down.'

I looked at the engine instruments: all three were still sitting at about 96 per cent. The captain's airspeed indicator was ridiculously low, like about 60 kt—which was about 60 kt below stall speed.

He continued: 'The autoslats are extending.' It was these that had caused the vibration.

Stalling? At 96 per cent? In normal unaccelerated level flight? It didn't make sense.

'We can't be stalling,' I said. 'Get the nose back up to about two or three degrees nose-up. There's something wrong with the speed indication.'

He kept the nose low, so I leant over him, removed his hand from the yoke and set the attitude at about three degrees nose up. As I recall, the indicated airspeed was very low, near zero.

I told him to hold that attitude while I found the autoslat circuit breaker, which I pulled out. This would stop the slat extensions.

A check of the overhead panel revealed that a pitot heat circuit breaker had popped. I reset it.

Calling the pilot by name I said, 'there's nothing wrong with the aeroplane or the engines. How many times have you said that power plus attitude equals performance?'

The indicated airspeed (IAS) soon returned to normal, but before long the circuit breaker popped again, and once again the IAS bled off.

During all this I do not remember referring to the standby instruments, nor what the co-pilot's instruments were doing.

During the altitude excursion, we hadn't made radio calls to any agency; the aircraft was slowly returned to its original flight level using the standby instruments.

We decided to divert the aircraft rather than fly on to Townsville with no IAS or autopilot.

We advised Oakland Centre that we had abnormal instrument indications and were diverting to Nauru. Some time later Oakland Centre advised that Nauru was refusing to accept the aircraft.

Discussion in the cockpit determined that Majuro, in the Marshall Islands, was probably the next best option. We advised Oakland and obtained a clearance direct to Majuro.

During late descent into Majuro the captain's airspeed returned to normal and the arrival was without any further incident.

On the ground, inspection revealed a circle of ice about 30–40mm radius around the angle-of-attack vane, which was frozen in position. This was evidently the cause of the autoslat operation.

The computer associated with the air data system was reset. The angle-of-attack ice then cleared. The popped circuit breakers were reset and stayed in. The aircraft continued to Townsville without further incident.

I sometimes wonder what might have happened if the pilot had not pulled the nose up to three degrees. Would he have done so if I hadn't made it to the cockpit?

No doubt a second or two later and the power levers would have been at idle. Analysis in that configuration would have been far more difficult, other than the fact that zero airspeed is an impossibility. It is interesting how the abnormal attracts attention and response, even when the abnormal is wrong.

The lesson from all of this? Power plus attitude equals performance. Never forget this. It's no mere equation, nor is it a cliché. Whether it's a Jabiru, an FA-18 or an A380, your combination of power setting and angle of attack will determine what the aircraft does. That's been true since the Wright brothers. It's the way aeroplanes fly, and the first thing to remember when your aeroplane appears to start flying strangely.

It's a formula that could have saved all on board Air France 447 in June 2009—had it been applied.

It is also interesting that when pilots are tested for an instrument rating, they are required to fly the aircraft on 'limited panel'. I wonder if this embeds an attitude that encourages greater faith on the least reliable instruments, the pitot-static pressure instruments. Failure of the attitude reference system is an almost unheard-of occurrence on glass cockpit aircraft. But loss of the pressure instruments can happen to the best and most reliable systems through causes such as sticky tape left over a static port, or a mud dauber wasp making its home in a pitot tube (both of these were involved in fatal air transport crashes). Maybe there is a case for limited panel to refer to loss of the pressure instruments.

NOTES:

CHAPTER 6

CONTROLLED AIRSPACE, AIR TRAFFIC CONTROL & AIRPORTS

"The Citation pilot got it wrong and the controller didn't pick up on the fact he got it wrong National Air Traffic Services has now changed its procedures on the way it communicates to the pilot..."

A Boeing 777 and Cessna Citation 525
In a 'near-miss' came within 200ft over
London, July 2009

ERCAN AIRSPACE

CHIRP

Feb 2017, Issue 121

For many years the airline industry has been transiting ERCAN Airspace (the boundary between Turkish and Nicosia Airspace). It would be true to say that this is a CRM/Human Factors issue that has continued for years and possibly illustrates the industry's indifference to act upon CRM issues.

There is confusion as to who/what ERCAN are or do; crews omit to contact the relevant or appropriate ATC service; crews accept ATC instructions from ERCAN in contradiction to Nicosia ATC instruction, etc. Air Safety Reports are a plenty with reference incidents at this airspace boundary. However due to 'politics' the industry has chosen to ignore what is a massive safety issue, which looks likely to be unresolved for many more years.

Lessons Learned:

Is it not time for the aviation industry to demand a resolution to this ATC issue?

CHIRP Comment: The issue raised in this report is a long-standing one. It is a risk factor that operators should address using their SMS; are operators prepared to tolerate the risk as it stands, mitigate the risk or stop using the airspace? This operator has confirmed that it has identified the issue of ERCAN advisory airspace as a deviation from normal ATC practices and as a result the difference creates a risk to the operation. This risk, like all ATC risks, is monitored by the Company. It is mitigated by promulgation of clear information to crews on who the controlling authority for each sector is. In seeking a resolution of the issue, the operator is one of a number that have raised it with the joint CAA and Department for Transport State Safety Partnership.

NOTES:

METROPLEX MYSTIQUE -
AIRPORTS & SHARED AIRSPACE

CALLBACK

A Metroplex is a metropolitan area that includes one or more commercial airports with complex, shared airspace and serves at least one major city. Potential benefits include reduced fuel burns, fewer aircraft exhaust emissions, and improved on-time performance.

The Optimized Profile Descent (OPD), the Optimization of Airspace and Procedures in the Metroplex (OAPM), and Time Based Flow Management (TBFM) are important pieces of the Metroplex concept. Operational problems that occur in Metroplex areas are not unique to Metroplex environments nor attributable to Metroplex mystique. Threats experienced in Metroplex areas result from complex interactions and forces at play when optimizing airspace, time, and aircraft operations. Some threats are exclusive to the Metroplex environment and relate directly to a piece of the Metroplex concept. Most threats are not limited strictly to the Metroplex environment, but they are intensified by the higher traffic density. ASRS reported incidents citing Metroplex issues reveal that the usual suspects are involved when considering related factors such as degraded communication, misunderstanding, lack of procedural knowledge, and poor execution.

Following are examples of reported Metroplex incidents from Pilot and Controller points of view. Resulting complications include traffic compression, aircraft separation, vectors for spacing, airspace violations, potential airborne conflicts, and airspeed reassignments that result in unachievable altitude restrictions.

SWEET SEPARATION

CALLBACK

June 2017, Issue 449

After receiving clearance for a visual approach, a Challenger Jet Captain was drawn into a compromising position. The incident illustrates a looming concern as Airport Acceptance Rates (AAR's) and Airport Departure Rates (ADR's) are increased within a Metroplex.

South of Avenal, ATC [vectored] a heavy B747 1,000 feet above us, sequencing us behind them for Runway 24L with repeated cautions for wake turbulence. Both aircraft were instructed to fly heading 065 after Santa Monica, which puts them on a downwind for Runway 24L. The B747 had made the turn to final when ATC asked us if we had a visual on the B747. We acknowledged that we did and were cleared for the visual. At that point, separation from terrain and other aircraft is now my responsibility. We set up for a squared off base to final turn to maximize wake turbulence separation from the heavy B747. Before we intercepted the final approach course, the Final Controller issued us a heading of 230 degrees. This shortened our turn to final and reduced our separation from the B747. After the

B747 touched down, Tower cleared a Super A380 into position on Runway 24L and then subsequently cleared him for takeoff. We had minimum traffic separation from that aircraft and zero wake turbulence separation. A follow-up call to the Tower revealed that although ATC has guidelines of 5 miles minimum separation between departing aircraft and the same standard for arriving aircraft, there is no standard separation between a departing aircraft and an arriving aircraft.

NOTES:

WAKING UP DURING THE
DESCENT - C560XL

CALLBACK

June 2017, Issue 449

This C560XL Captain was a bit upset when he encountered the wake of another aircraft. The two aircraft were descending within a Metroplex on different STARs that serve different airports, share common waypoints, and provide guidance to aircraft whose weights could differ by two orders of magnitude.

While flying the FERN5 arrival into Santa Monica, descending thru FL370, we experienced severe wake turbulence from another aircraft in front of us. I believe [the aircraft was] a Super A380, on the SADDE6 arrival to Los Angeles. The event took place between REBRG and DERBB intersections with ATC reporting that the Super A380 was 15 nautical miles ahead of us and descending. The aircraft upset was an abrupt negative g's, followed immediately by a right roll to 90+ degrees.... I quickly brought the plane back to a level attitude, assessed passenger injuries, aircraft control in approach/landing configurations, and whether any structural damage [had occurred]. [There were] no serious injuries, and aircraft integrity was verified. We continued to our destination due to close proximity of all diverts (Van Nuys, Burbank, and Los Angeles). We [advised ATC of a medical issue with a passenger], and as a precaution, to have the passenger checked out by medical personnel upon arrival....

The FERN5 and SADDE6 [arrivals] converge and share fixes DERBB, REYES and FILLMORE. No altitude restrictions exist [at these three fixes] on either arrival. The FERN5 is tailored for smaller General Aviation (GA) aircraft and the SADDE6 tends to be for larger commercial aircraft. These two arrivals should not converge or share fixes, and [they should] have altitude crossing restrictions. ATC should also be aware of these conflicts and not allow Heavies [and] Supers to be descending thru this airspace [without] much, much greater lateral and vertical separation.

NOTES:

CONTROL THE BALL

CALLBACK

June 2017, Issue 449

An Approach Controller experienced unpredictable compression and inadequate spacing that resulted from new procedures and an OPD serving the Atlanta Metroplex. He offers his analysis, rationale, and solution.

While assisting another Controller on the combined TAR-D/L position, four arrivals were inbound from the northeast, two on the WINNG arrival and two on the PECHY arrival. All aircraft needed to be blended in order to fit on the base leg for Runway 26R. Aircraft X, the lead aircraft on the PECHY arrival, was followed by Aircraft Y, also on the PECHY arrival. The spacing provided by Center was more than the required 5 miles, but due to the overtake created by the fact that arrivals cross the airspace boundary at 280 knots "descending via" the arrival procedure, this spacing rapidly collapsed to less than 5 miles. To mitigate the situation, the Controller issued Aircraft Y 210 knots to increase spacing enough to give the Final Controller something to work with. Aircraft Y immediately responded that they would no longer be able to meet their altitude restrictions if they slowed, which would, in turn, result in an airspace violation of satellite and departure airspace.

It is unacceptable to get aircraft at 280 knots on the base leg, with unpredictable compression (there is a 15 mile window in which the Pilot can slow to 250 knots), especially when two base leg feeds are routinely fed to the same runway. Many times it is inappropriate to feed the Final Controller at a speed greater than 210 knots (our facility standard operating procedures specifically state that the final should not normally be fed at speeds greater than 210 knots), and aircraft "descending via" are unable to make altitude restrictions if slowed beyond the 280/250 knot restrictions on the Optimum Profile Descent arrival procedures.

[We should] terminate the OPD procedures at [our airspace] boundary and have all aircraft level at hard altitudes and in trail at 250 knots, especially when feeding dual base legs. The OPD is manageable in a single stream scenario, but we are being fed dual stream OPD arrivals from the northeast and the northwest. This complexity...creates a huge safety risk. Simply slowing an aircraft to 210 knots to comply with our SOP results in the aircraft not being able to meet crossing restrictions, [which then] results in multiple airspace violations.... The dual arrivals are routinely blended into a single base leg feed, requiring additional speed control and vectors. This procedure is not acceptable.

NOTES:

OLD HABITS DIE HARD

CALLBACK

June 2017, Issue 449

An unexpected pilot route deviation prompted this Controller to issue a new "direct to" and "descend via" clearance. All seemed in order until the Controller remembered that the new OPD STAR is not what it used to be.

Center cleared this aircraft direct SMOOV and failed to enter it into Enroute Automation Modernization (ERAM) (ERAM showed the aircraft routed over the HOWRR transition for the SMOOV arrival). I eventually noticed that the aircraft was not flying the route I expected it to fly, and that's when I had to figure out how to clear him back onto the route and issue a "descend via" clearance. So I [cleared] him direct SMOOV and issued the "descend via" clearance, but I had forgotten that the crossing restriction for SMOOV is at or above 10,000 feet. It had been 12,000 feet for ages before these new Optimal Profile Descent arrivals. The aircraft descended early down to 10,000 feet into A80 (Atlanta) Macon sector's airspace before crossing the boundary for the new shelf which has been set aside for this descent. There was no loss of separation or conflict.

[At or above] 10,000 feet at Transfer of Control Point (TCP) SMOOV is a terrible design. It dramatically increases complexity and Controller phraseology in any situation where an aircraft isn't flying the entire arrival as published. Today, it was because a prior Controller in Jacksonville ARTCC cleared the aircraft direct SMOOV even though they're not supposed to. During thunderstorm season, there will be many times when aircraft will be deviating off of the published route for the STAR. The TCP, SMOOV, should be changed to at or above 11,000 feet, at the very least, thus totally eliminating any risk of an aircraft descending too soon into approach airspace without excessive verbiage from the Controller.

NOTES:

CHAPTER 7

TECHNOLOGY & AUTOMATION

**"What is the cause of most aviation accidents:
Usually it is because someone does too much too
soon, followed very quickly by too little too late."**
Steve Wilson
NTSB investigator
Oshkosh, WI
August, 1996

RNAV (AREA NAVIGATION) PROBLEMS

CALLBACK

With the improvement of navigational capabilities, Area Navigation (RNAV) and Required Navigation Performance (RNP) operations have become routine procedures for performing many terminal instrument approaches. RNAV and RNP together compose Performance Based Navigation (PBN), which uses satellites and onboard equipment for navigation procedures that are more precise and accurate than standard avionics and ground-based navigation aids. PBN is so named because the types of routes and procedures an aircraft can fly are dependent upon the performance level of equipment and pilot training. RNAV permits aircraft to fly any desired flight path within the coverage of ground-based or space-based navigation aids, within the limits of aircraft avionics, or with a combination of these. RNP is a more advanced form of RNAV that includes an onboard performance monitoring and alerting capability.

The use of RNAV and RNP terminal approach procedures has grown. As of Publication Cycle 01/05/2017, the FAA Instrument Flight Procedures (IFP) Inventory Summary lists a total of 6,837 RNAV charts comprising 14,932 unique sets of approach minimums.

With expanded use of these procedures, new problems and concerns arise.

ASRS receives reports that indicate pilots experience common RNAV problems. While RNAV technology may be relatively new and still evolving, a large portion of reported problems appear to have roots in the basic knowledge and fundamentals of instrument flight. The following reports depicting issues that crews encounter with RNAV operations in the terminal environment.

THE UNEXPECTED RNAV EXCURSION – BACK TO BASICS I

CALLBACK

Feb 2017, Issue 445

This air carrier crew entered the RNAV approach that they intended to fly into their FMS. An unexpected turn during the approach started the next unwelcome turn of events.

I was the pilot flying. The pilot monitoring had loaded the full RNAV (GPS) RWY 34R approach. After being cleared for the approach, we got established on the inbound course. Without notification the aircraft began a right turn. Realizing that the aircraft had begun to turn, we disconnected the autopilot and attempted hand flying the aircraft back onto course. Realizing that I was descending, I began to increase power and climb the aircraft. In the descent, a TERRAIN WARNING aural alert sounded, and a go-around and missed approach were initiated. Storms in the area had created a very high workload. The turn was caused by a full procedure turn that had been included during the FMS setup for the approach that should not have been there. The excessive descent was caused by a work overload for myself as the pilot flying.

NOTES:

THE UNPROTECTED RNAV DESCENT – BACK TO BASICS II

CALLBACK

Feb 2017, Issue 445

This aircrew experienced a late approach change that required them to program an RNAV approach. Manually reprogramming that approach resulted in an undesirable flight condition in weather and mountainous terrain.

We were filed to fly the MQU1A arrival into SKBO. Prior to MQU, the FO listened to ATIS and reported landings to Runways 13L and 13R. We briefed the ILS Runway 13L approach.... Approaching 14,000 feet,...the Approach Controller assigned 250 knots and the RNAV (GNSS) RWY 13R approach. We were also cleared direct to NEPOP. At this point I felt slightly rushed.

I loaded the RNAV (GNSS) RWY 13R approach, selected the NEPOP transition,...and briefed the approach. It was in the box as follows: Line 1 - NEPOP procedural hold at 13,000 feet; Line 2 - NEPOP at 12,000 feet; Line 3 - URULO (FAF) at 10,000 feet; Line 4 - RWY 13R.

Knowing that the Controller did not expect us to enter a

procedural hold at NEPOP, I attempted to line select Line 2 (NEPOP at 12,000 feet) to Line 1. The box did not allow that action. At this time I elected to concentrate on slowing the airplane down for the approach. I directed the FO to...correct the sequence of waypoints for the intended approach. The FO thought he had solved the problem by line selecting Line 3 (URULO) to Line 2. This action displayed the proper sequence of NEPOP followed by URULO. By this time the aircraft was in the approach mode.... When VNAV was selected, VNAV PATH was displayed in the FMA. Thinking the approach was correctly sequenced, I directed the FO to set 9,100 in the MCP altitude window. The autopilot was on and soon...started a slow descent. Within a few hundred feet we broke out of the clouds. ... We saw the airport and all surrounding terrain.... I suspected we were low...based on visual cues. The aircraft gave an ALTITUDE and PULL UP WARNING as we passed over a ridge. I elected to not respond to these warnings since I had visual contact on all terrain. We proceeded to Runway 13R and made a normal landing.... I now believe when URULO was line selected to Line 2, we lost the altitude protection of 12,000 feet at NEPOP.

NOTES:

THE DUBIOUS RNAV DESCENT –
BACK TO BASICS III

CALLBACK

Feb 2017, Issue 445

Confusion over RNAV Instrument Approach Procedures and RNAV FMS displays allowed this corporate crew to descend below published altitudes during their RNAV approach. The result was another close encounter with terra firma.

The airport reported 10 miles visibility and 900 feet scattered clouds, and the approach occurred during dusk while the sun was setting. We originally planned and briefed the visual approach with the LOC DME RWY 28L backup utilizing the FMS. The LOC DME RWY 28L was [reported out of service in the] NOTAMS. Approaching WIGGL, the IAF for both approaches, ATC informed us that we needed to choose an actual approach, as the airport weather had changed to 10 miles visibility in smoke and 900 feet overcast. We asked for...the RNAV (GPS) Y RWY 28L and decided to forgo a thorough briefing and fly it with the PM guiding the Pilot Flying (PF). Unfortunately, we missed the step down fixes between the FAF and the MAP that were not represented in the FMS. There was slight confusion in the application of the step down fixes, i.e. [whether they] apply to only the LP minimums, or also to the LNAV minimums.

I decided to descend to the MDA as early as possible to allow for more time to search for the runway in the haze. During the level off at the MDA,...about 6 nautical miles from the runway and descending through about 1,250 feet, we received an EGPWS TERRAIN CAUTION followed immediately by an EGPWS TERRAIN WARNING. We immediately initiated the escape manoeuvre. We were still in VMC conditions and some distance from the runway.... Still able to remain within the "stable criteria," we elected to level off at about 1,500 to 1,600 feet. We were clear of the EGPWS CAUTION and WARNING areas, with no audio messages and no colors depicted on the terrain map, so we continued with the descent to level off at the MDA about 3 nautical miles from the runway. At that point we saw the runway and made an uneventful approach and landing.

NOTES:

COMMON RNAV AUTOMATION
SYNDROME

CALLBACK

Feb 2017, Issue 445

A change in runway and approach type required this B737 crew to program an RNAV approach and link it to the active arrival. It proved problematic, as did Electronic Flight Bag (EFB) currency, in executing the RNAV approach.

The current ATIS information listed the ILS for Runways 16C and 16R in use.... The ILS for 16R had been set up and briefed. After checking in with Seattle Approach, we were instructed to fly the RNAV (RNP) Z RWY 16C approach, which joined with the... arrival.... The Captain attempted to re-program the FMS for the new approach.... I discovered that I did not have access to the approach since...I did not perform an update on my EFB on the layover. The Captain...had updated his EFB...and did have access to the approach, so we agreed that I would brief and fly from his approach plate. In the attempt to re-program the RNAV approach in the FMC and prepare to brief, the correct sequence of waypoints along the...arrival... dropped out of the LEGS page in the FMC, and a discontinuity was created after the waypoint...directly in front of us. I had requested that the Pilot Monitoring (PM) clean up the LEGS page prior to executing the change, however this did not happen due to the high workload...on the PM at that time. Consequently, when the aircraft traversed the next waypoint and reached a discontinuity on the LEGS page, it sequenced out of LNAV and into Control Wheel Steering (CWS). We immediately saw the change and attempted to turn toward the next waypoint, correct the discontinuity, and re-engage the correct lateral navigation. We reached a lateral excursion of 1.45 [NM] prior to correcting back to the published course. ATC queried us about our lateral excursion..., and we advised them of our correction.... We continued the arrival and were re-assigned the ILS 16C approach without further event.

NOTES:

HOW LOW SHOULD YOU GO - B737

CALLBACK

Sept 2016, Issue 440

This B737 Crew encountered a ramp hazard that is not uncommon, but got a surprise that grounded the aircraft, in part, because local authorities had altered the airport facility.

From the Captain's report:

We were cleared to descend via the arrival landing south. As the Pilot Monitoring (PM), I set the lowest altitude on that STAR, which was 6,000 feet, and...then accidentally abrogated my PM duties by not stating, "I'll set the next lowest altitude of FL220," as we approached [the altitude restricted fix] in Level Change pitch mode. Already high on the profile and well above crossing restrictions, it wasn't of immediate concern, but [it was] completely improper procedure on my part. Instead of correcting that, I passed the radios to the First Officer as I took to the [public address (PA) system] to offer a good-bye to our customers.

[After I finished] with the PA, I reported, "Back on number 1 radio," to the First Officer, who had switched us to Approach but had not yet checked in. I...checked in and reported, "Descending via the... arrival." I did not refer to the Primary Flight Display (PFD) to check what pitch mode we were in, but the Controller said, "Climb and maintain 10,000 feet." We were on a STAR, and this was such an unusual call.... I said, "Say again," and the Controller unemotionally repeated, "Climb and maintain 10,000 feet." We complied immediately. By that time I saw that the bottom [altitude] window of the next fix showed 10,000. The Controller then asked, "Why were you down at 6,000 feet?" I said, "My bust," as there was no excuse for this performance.

I had been relying on the VNAV automation instead of the old fashioned, "Set the next lowest altitude," which forces both pilots [to be] situationally aware with respect to the profile. I was allured by the pure beauty of a clear Spring day and was obviously much less aware than I needed to be.

From the First Officer's report:

The Captain set 6,000 feet into the MCP altitude window, and we both verified it against the bottom altitude of the arrival.... The Captain [reported to Approach Control] that we were descending via the arrival. At this point I simply was not looking at our displays and a very short time later, we were told to climb to 10,000 feet from our current altitude of 6,000 feet.... I knew right away that we never got back into VNAV path for protection.

NOTES:

TEETERING ON THE APPROACH - GULFSTREAM

CALLBACK

Sept 2016, Issue 440

A Gulfstream Captain, experiencing strong winds during an approach, became fixated on the automation's correction. He then lost sight of his own situation and the airport.

During the arrival into Teterboro, we were cleared for the ILS to Runway 6. The Pilot in Command (PIC) let the autopilot drift left of the center line and [I told him] that the airport was in sight at one o'clock. The PIC's comment was, "Look at how much correction this thing is putting in." We continued to drift left. I told him again that the center line was to the right and that the airport was in sight. The PIC turned right and started to descend. Then he said that he had lost sight of the [airport]. I told him that the airport was at eleven o'clock and that he was way too low for where we were. I [pointed out] the towers south of [the airport] to him twice. He then said he had them and asked where the stadium was. At this time the tower came on the frequency and gave us a low altitude alert. The airport was at our ten o'clock position, but at this point, I lost sight of the airport and told the PIC to go around. At that point, we both picked up the airport visually and landed without further incident.

The trip was extremely rough and had been for the preceding 20 minutes. The wind at 4,000 feet was out of the northwest at 65 knots. The [reported] landing wind was from 330 [degrees] at 19 [knots, gusting to] 25 [knots]. This [is] a classic example of how automation dependency can cause a very experienced pilot to lose track of situational awareness and ignore the basics of flying the aircraft.

NOTES:

A DESCENDING STAR - GULFSTREAM

CALLBACK

Sept 2016, Issue 440

A Gulfstream aircrew was given two runway changes during the arrival, and the automation did not quite lead them down the correct vertical path.

The FMS was programmed with the arrival, and VNAV was selected. All seemed well as we descended to, and crossed, HOMRR at 16,000 feet and 250 knots. However, the next fix, VNNOM, required crossing between 11,000 feet and 10,000 feet. VNNOM is 4.1 nautical miles from HOMRR. Crossing HOMRR at 16,000 feet, we realized that it was almost impossible to lose 5,000 to 6,000 feet in 4.1 nautical miles. At this point I clicked off the automation and pointed the nose down, achieving a descent rate of better than 6,000 feet per minute. Our airspeed increased to 280 knots, and we crossed VNNOM high and fast.

The STAR called for crossing HOMRR at or below 16,000 feet, and the FMS should have been in a position to make the next subsequent fix. Obviously we could have done a better job monitoring the situation.... We made, programmed, and verified two runway and approach changes during this descent prior to HOMRR. In fact, the first change went from a landing east flow to a landing west flow. This could actually explain why the FMS logic chose 16,000 feet at HOMRR instead of lower.... Landing east on the EAGUL FIVE requires crossing [the next fix] immediately past HOMRR between 15,000 feet and 14,000 feet.

This is a really poorly designed STAR. Something should be done to warn other aircrews not to fall into the same trap.

NOTES:

THE VIRTUAL GREEN FLASH

CALLBACK

Sept 2016, Issue 440

Automation dependency also exists in the ATC environment. A Center Controller, while using an automated hand-off procedure, "flashed" several aircraft to incorrect sectors. This alert Controller noticed the problem, bypassed the automation, and minimized the airspace violation.

I was working Sector XX, R-Side and D-Side combined. Traffic was moderately busy and we had overflights available through the [airspace] which [adds] some complexity. I was flashing several aircraft to Approach to initiate our flash-through procedure. The automation forwarded the handoffs [incorrectly] to Sector YYG instead of YYB. [Initially,] I did not notice that in my scan, and one of the aircraft penetrated [the adjacent sector's] boundary without a handoff having been completed. I called Sector YYB for the late point-out and redirected the [automated, incorrect] handoff from Sector YYG to YYB. The Controller there took the handoff and flashed it on to Sector ZZ.

This is a repeated problem with YY Approach's automation. I would recommend their automation be forwarded correctly so the appropriate sector sees the handoff flashing at them.

NOTES:

MORE THAN MEETS THE EYE - B737

CALLBACK

Sept 2016, Issue 440

This B737 aircrew trusted their automation to calculate the descent point, but they did not consider the winds. The situation was compounded as a second problem resulted from the action they took to solve the first.

From the First Officer's report:

[We were] given the crossing restriction 10 [miles] north of HIELY at 13,000 feet. [I] got behind on the descent, asked for relief, and the Controller gave us a heading and a descent to 13,000 feet. [We] entered moderate chop, and I over sped [the aircraft about] 5 knots or so [in the] clean configuration. I was...rushing to comply, and, along with chop, I got behind the aircraft. I need to do a better job cross checking the automation against what the restrictions actually are. I was trusting in the automation too much for when to start my descent.

From the Captain's report:

[Our mistake was] over reliance on the automation for planning the descent. [We should have] double checked that it makes sense with the winds and should have been more aware of speed control when using vertical speed to try to comply with a crossing restriction.

AUTOMATING COMPLACENCY

CALLBACK

Mar 2017, Issue 446

A G-V pilot was surprised when his automation did not capture the altitude as it always had. Contemplating the incident, he discovered the underlying problem.

I was given a clearance to cross an arrival intersection at 14,000 feet. I reset the altitude alerter to 14,000 feet and selected VPATH for the vertical mode of operation. The autopilot was [engaged in] the descent mode.... The Pilot Not Flying (PNF), was out of the seat to use the lavatory prior to landing. All was in order, so I looked at the FMS to review the ATIS information and to further review the arrival.... During this time my attention was diverted from the primary flight display. The automation did not...capture the assigned altitude. It kept descending until I looked and saw the altimeter at 13,300 feet. I immediately disconnected the autopilot and auto throttles and corrected the aircraft back to 14,000 feet as assigned. As I was leveling at 14,000 feet, the PNF returned to his station and asked me what had happened. A short exchange took place, and we pressed on with the flight. No instruction or challenge was made by ATC, and no conflict was indicated by the TCAS.

For a long...time after this flight concluded, I evaluated the performance of my duties.... I failed to adequately monitor the specific flight path of the aircraft during a critical time in the flight. I got complacent..., and I believe it was because for so many years of operating this equipment, never had the automation failed to perform as it had been set up. I believed that it would do as always.... I allowed myself to occupy my attention with other aspects of the flight. Worse, I allowed this to happen when the other pilot was away from his station. I did not discipline myself to avoid distraction from the primary duty.... Complacency contributed directly to this deviation and...has no place on the flight deck.

NOTES:

DESCENT BELOW DESIGNATED ALTITUDE

CHIRP

Aug 2017, Issue 123

We were on arrival into [an airport in the London TMA] from Belgium. While on arrival we were with London Control and given an assigned heading which took us off the assigned STAR. This is not unusual as we rarely stay on the assigned Arrivals and Departures when with London Control. I was given a descent on our present heading to FL100. I set 10000 in our altitude selector and continued an approx. 1500 fpm descent. During that time my Co Captain, Pilot Monitoring, was off frequency communicating with [handling agent] in preparation for our arrival. We were issued a frequency change to a new sector and we checked in. We were next issued a turn direct to [ ] and were continuing to descend to FL100. Around FL103 the controller called and asked what we were doing. My colleague responded, going direct to [ ]. The controller said, no you were assigned FL110. Our response was to ask if he wanted us to climb. He responded no continue descent to FL90.

Lessons Learned:

Well the obvious answer is to always check and double check altitude assignments. In this case ATC had several chances to catch the mistake, if it was a mistake. I repeated what I thought to be our assigned altitude to two different controllers. ATC also has the capability to see what I have in my altitude selector so it shouldn't have been a surprise that I was descending to FL100. The Arrival phase into the London Area is an extremely busy and complex time. We always need to be vigilant to maintain a high level of situational awareness. In the US, ATC has adopted much less of a "positive control" concept for arrival flow. Aircraft are metered using the arrivals which aids in reducing errors and increasing flow. It would be great to see a more effective arrival airway system in the UK.

CHIRP Comment: We are grateful for this honest account of an incident from which there are several lessons for the benefit of other pilots. In essence, a simple error was not detected or corrected by the barriers which might otherwise have prevented a level bust. The RT tapes record that the crew was instructed to descend to FL110 to be level by [ ]. This was correctly read back but FL100 was selected in the autopilot and the aircraft began to descend. The incorrect level was challenged by ATC as the aircraft was descending past FL103. No other aircraft were affected by this level bust and the controller immediately cleared the aircraft to FL90.

The erroneous selection of FL100 selected altitude was a typical and common example of a human performance error: a correct read back but an incorrect action. One of the barriers for catching this type of error is monitoring by the other pilot. Unfortunately he was speaking to the handling agent when the ATC descent clearance was issued and read back correctly by the handling pilot. Although FL100 is typically the level below which flight decks go sterile, many operators use FL200 for operations into the London TMA because the airspace is so busy and complex. If it is essential for one pilot to go off the operating frequency below FL200 and a descent is instructed while they are away, on their return they should ask ATC to confirm the altitude cleared; this is not uncommon and controllers would prefer to be asked for confirmation than risk a level bust.

Another potential barrier was the downlink of the altitude selected in the aircraft FMS. However, the controller did not detect the incorrect altitude selected by the pilot and pilots should not expect them to do so. Controllers are not mandated to check the selected altitude because it would be impractical given the amount of traffic in the TMA and the variable delay that occurs between clearing aircraft to descend and the altitude being selected. If controllers do see a discrepancy they will try to resolve it, but it is not currently practical to expect them to do so routinely. In future controllers will increasingly make use of electronic flight strips (rather than the paper ones) and these, in some situations, will alert the controller if there is a discrepancy between the cleared altitude and the Mode S indication. Unfortunately, the utility of the selected altitude function may not be compatible with RNP procedures and step-climb SIDs. Therefore, while technical solutions will be welcome and beneficial, from a human factors perspective the old adage – 'never assume, check' – comes to mind in circumstances such as occurred here.

Once again, kudos to the reporter for providing the opportunity to highlight some important lessons.

NOTES:

SEEING THINGS - PILATUS PC-12

CASA

Aug 14, 2017

An incident on an aircraft equipped with a synthetic vision system raises unsettling questions about technology, insidious failure and tunnel vision.

Half past one, on a June morning at Meekatharra airport. Dead of night and just about the coldest hour of the entire year in this sunbaked inland West Australian town, but at least the moon is shining. A Pilatus PC-12 of the Royal Flying Doctor Service is undergoing pre take-off checks for a retrieval flight to Paraburdoo. Among the single engine turboprop's advanced features is synthetic vision. A synthetic vision system is an aircraft cockpit display that presents the environment around the aircraft using computer-generated imagery recreated from its navigation database to create a picture of terrain on the primary flight display. It uses GPS to paint the terrain on the attitude indicator.

The aircraft has been hangared and its GPS units have to reacquire the satellites overhead in the clear sky. The pilot pauses the aircraft before the threshold to let this happen. GPS 1 locates all its satellites as required, but GPS 2 fails to initialise and shows a caution message UNABLE FMS-GPS MON, on its display. The pilot flying reaches for the quick reference handbook and in it finds a fix for the problem. The caution message clears and the aircraft lifts off about 0145 local time with both systems operational.

About 18 seconds later, it gets weird. As the aircraft is climbing through about 250 feet AGL at an airspeed of about 110 knots, the radio altimeter (radalt) winds down to zero. The radalt low altitude awareness display rises to meet the altitude readout.

The synthetic vision image on both pilots' primary flight displays (PFDs) shows they are sideslipping while sinking to the ground. The runway is darting left and off the screen, as the ground representation is rising rapidly up to meet the zero pitch reference line.

The pilot flying pulls back on the control column; flight data retrieved later shows the flight path indicator moved up to about 15 degrees. But there are no warnings sounding or cautions lighting. The stick shaker does not activate because the aircraft is nowhere near the angle of attack it would be at the PC-12's quite impressive stall speed of 67 knots. Most strangely, there is no word from the terrain aware- ness and warning system (TAWS).

The check pilot looks outside (there is no standby instrument on the right side of the cockpit), sees a faint but visible horizon in the moonlight and says 'attitude!' causing the pilot to focus to the standby instrument, monitoring its old-style flat horizon and its speed and alti- tude tapes. It shows the aircraft climbing, but nose-high.

Airspeed, which had reduced to 101 knots increases to the planned 110 knots, and at about 850 feet the synthetic vision returns to normal and the rest of the flight is entirely placid, at least as far as the recording equipment is concerned. The crew report the incident.

The Australian Transport Safety Bureau (ATSB) investigation determined that both antennas associated with the radalt system (one for transmit and one for receive) had failed, after more than 9000 hours in service. 'The antennas did not have a life limit, but were required to be replaced "on condition", which essentially meant that the antennas remained in service until they failed,' the ATSB said.

The pilots were both experienced, able to put their incident into the context of thousands of hours, and reported in detail to the ATSB. They told the investigator this experience was different to previous instrument failures, which they had both experienced. It was harder to compensate for, paradoxically, because in normal use synthetic vision worked very well.

The ATSB report stated, 'Both pilots commented that they had previously experienced failure of primary flight instruments at low level and at night in different aircraft (without synthetic vision systems). They had been able to disregard the erroneous or failed instruments and reference the standby instruments to maintain control of the aircraft and situational awareness. However, the prominence of the synthetic vision display is such that it is difficult to ignore erroneous information and locate valid information. Additionally, the pilot flying reported feeling a level motion sickness, probably associated with the combined effects of the prominent synthetic vision display and conflicting vestibular sensory information.'

The maker of the display, Honeywell, issued Pilot Advisory Letter PAL-APEX-01 to all pilots, chief pilots and flight operations managers on 11 August 2016. It advised pilots that synthetic vision was for situational awareness, and should not be used for indicating attitude or altitude in lieu of the primary flight display indications for pitch, roll, yaw or altitude.

CASA human factors specialist, Reuben Delamore, says further instructions and admonishments aimed at pilots are at best only part of the solution. They do not address underlying issues of technology, psychology and design.

'We've got all this fabulous technology on flight decks, but with hindsight, as an industry, we're not necessarily considering what could happen if technology doesn't behave as expected. All we have is a general principle—technologies that work in new ways fail in new ways,' he says.

Delamore notes a long standing design issue in the form of the cautionary placard on the aircraft's panel. 'The synthetic vision system had a little placard below its screen that said words to the effect of "don't use this as your primary means of information,"' he says.

The placard was there because as a non-redundant system without self-monitoring, synthetic vision can only be used as an aid to situational awareness.

This is at odds with the fact that vision is our primary sense, Delamore says. 'When a visual representation is provided that appears accurate, of course we will attend to that information to the point where it will become relied upon, despite the designers' placard.'

The placard was an example of trying to solve a system problem, in this case the unknown (although relatively good) reliability of the synthetic vision system, by placing the onus on the user.

'Signage is the least useful control,' Delamore says. 'It's a stopgap, and often a sign of poor design. The most common examples are doors that have to have push and pull written on them, to show you what to do.'

Delamore notes that synthetic vision systems are available at minimal cost as software for tablet computers and that the technology is becoming popular in sport aviation.

'Performance is considered, but speaking to users in sport aviation I have noticed a presumption that "the manufacturer's considered that so it will be OK." The other issue regarding tablet-based systems is the potential for users to "get buried in the menus",' he says.

The marketing-driven incentive for display manufacturers to offer more options and features is not necessarily in the interests of safety, Delamore says. 'This is often a trap, as it then requires a level of understanding to navigate the menus that may not be very clear to the user or takes time in using the system to learn.'

The potential issues with synthetic vision were foreseen early. In

2002, researchers Micah Endsley and William Jones listed several potential pitfalls:

Difficulty in correctly perceiving the vertical flight profile in a 3D display

The compelling influence of graphical 3D displays may over-come digitally presented instrument data, leaving the pilot open to spatial disorientation

The potential to believe no traffic (or other obstacles) is present if not displayed, when in fact this 'false world' could result from a data-base or sensor limitation.

They went on to say, 'Although the veridical nature of the synthetic vision's system display is its strong point—integrated infor-mation presented in a very natural manner—this also is its Achilles' heel. It is a far more compelling display than any previously and more likely to suck pilots into any false or ambiguous information it presents.'

A NASA study from 2009, the year in which the first certified synthetic vision system was installed on a Gulfstream business jet said, 'Will realistic terrain cause the pilot to focus on the artificial display to the exclusion of the outside world and backup instru-ments? Will synthetic vision displays be compelling and induce complacency?'

Delamore notes there was, thankfully, no complacency in the Meekathara incident, but the pilots said themselves that things could have been different if they had been tired, rather than on the first flight after a good rest.

NOTES:

CHAPTER 8

ON THE GROUND

"Flying is inherently dangerous. We like to gloss that over with clever rhetoric and comforting statistics, but these facts remain: gravity is constant and powerful, and speed kills. In combination, they are particularly destructive."
Dan Manningham
Business and Commercial
Aviation magazine

RAMP HAZARDS INTRODUCTION

CALLBACK

Airport ramp safety and associated hazards continually appear as common concerns with reported ramp events range from routine to remarkable, while the hazards and associated threats may exist almost anywhere. Many hazards are familiar, while others are uncommon. They can be obvious or concealed, and are often unexpected. Unmitigated ramp hazards frequently result in significant property damage or injury to personnel.

The routine tasks and interactions required during ramp operations may combine to produce unique circumstances and peculiar threats. Recognizing the hazards and identifying the threats requires anticipation, attention to detail, and situational awareness to avoid incidents when hazards develop or already exist.

Included is a cross section of ramp experiences. These excerpts illustrate a variety of ramp hazards that can be present. They describe the incidents that resulted and applaud the "saves" made by the Flight Crews and Ground Personnel involved.

A DOSE OF SAND AND FOD - B737

CALLBACK

Aug 2016, Issue 439

This B737 Crew encountered a ramp hazard that is not uncommon, but got a surprise that grounded the aircraft, in part, because local authorities had altered the airport facility.

[Our] aircraft arrived...and a normal exterior inspection was conducted with no abnormalities noted. There was a significant increase in wind strength directly behind the aircraft causing a dust storm.... Shortly after [the storm], a Ramp Agent informed us of... debris in both the intake and exhaust sections of both engines. The debris consisted of dust, sand, and small particles of stone.... The total quantity was estimated between one-fourth and one-half cup in each engine's exhaust section and about the same...in [each engine's] intake.

Dispatch and Maintenance Control were consulted and contract maintainers were summoned. Debris was vacuumed out of all sections of the engines and inspections noted no other visible defects. The engines were then [run] at idle power for five minutes with no abnormalities noted from the flight deck engine instruments. Visual inspection of the engines, unfortunately, indicated that additional debris had been expelled from the hot section...during engine spool down. Maintenance Control...grounded the aircraft pending a borescope inspection.... There is certainly a significant cost to this incident.

The airport authority had recently replaced all of the infield grass and areas between the runways and taxiways with a sand and gravel mix.... I am certain this is the material that found its way into the engines. I am astonished more aircraft have not fallen victim to this hazard.

NOTES:

GETTING CAUGHT UP AT WORK

CALLBACK

Aug 2016, Issue 439

This Lead Ramp Agent, while striving for excellence in the performance of his duties, was surprisingly pulled in another direction. His co-worker likely prevented a serious injury.

From the Lead Ramp Agent's report:

An Agent who was loading mail with me in the pit saw the lavatory service technician driving his equipment. He thought he was driving under the aircraft. I leaned [out] to see and...that is when my badge caught between the belt and the belt loader ramp and dragged my vest in.

I yelled and the other Agent pushed the emergency stop. Many thanks to the Agent who did what he did to prevent any injury.

From the co-worker Ramp Agent's report:

[While the flight was being serviced], I was in...the rear cargo hold [working] with the assistance of my Lead Ramp Agent. He...leaned over the end of the belt loader to check on a lavatory service truck that appeared to be under the aircraft fuselage. I heard him yell and turned to see his badge and vest caught between the baggage belt and the roller on the loader, and his face and chest [were] being pulled into the belt. I immediately hit the e-stop button and the belt stopped. Another Ramp Agent ran over...and turned off the belt loader key. We released the Lead's badge lanyard and vest from his neck and the other Agent restarted the belt. [The belt would not reverse, so] we... passed his badge through the same way it was pulled in.

NOTES:

RE-ENERGIZING EARLY - CRJ-700

CALLBACK

Aug 2016, Issue 439

This CRJ-700 Captain received a surprise after he blocked in and noticed that he was being refuelled even before the engines were shut down.

The aircraft was operating without an APU due to a MEL [item]. Ground power and air were requested on the in-range call. Upon arrival at our gate, the left engine was shut down and the hand signal was given to the Ground Lead for ground power. The individual acknowledged with a nod. During this time the aircraft beacon was on. After several minutes waiting for ground power, I noticed on the EICAS that the fueler had hooked up to the aircraft. I immediately shut down the aircraft and went to emergency power. I went out to speak with the supervisor.... I explained the importance of stopping an unsafe action and keeping personnel clear of the number 2 engine. Further, I explained how dangerous it was to attempt to fuel an aircraft while an engine is running and with passengers on the aircraft.

NOTES:

MISSED COMMUNICATIONS – AGAIN - B777

CALLBACK

Aug 2016, Issue 439

At the conclusion of his pushback, a B777 Captain received the "clear" signal that was clearly premature. The result was a taxi route that could have been presumed unobstructed, but was actually blocked by the tug.

After pushback from [the] gate, the tug driver asked me to set brakes. I did. He then told me the tow bar was disconnected. I told him to disconnect [his headset]. Within seconds after the tow bar was disconnected from the aircraft, but while [the tug] was basically still directly under the nose of the aircraft and in front of the nose landing gear, the marshaller gave me the "all clear" free to taxi signal—even though the tug hadn't moved! I have written this up time after time and it seems to be getting worse, not better. Someone is going to get killed if SOP is not followed!

NOTES:

UNSAFE IN THE SAFETY ZONE

CALLBACK

Aug 2016, Issue 439

An Air Carrier Captain took evasive action while turning in to the gate when a ground vehicle ignored the right of way rules and sped through the safety zone.

[As I was] turning in to [the] gate, a ground operations vehicle crossed directly in front of our aircraft. The vehicle was moving right to left at a high rate of speed...through the safety zone and directly across the lead-in line. To avoid a collision, I aggressively applied maximum wheel brakes, bringing the aircraft to a violent stop. After the vehicle had cleared the safety zone, we taxied in to the gate normally.

NOTES:

BRIDGING THE GAP

CALLBACK

Aug 2016, Issue 439

This Air Carrier Crew was actively taking precautions and mitigating risk as they taxied to the gate. Just when they thought the flight was all but over, an unexpected, uncommon, and unnoticed threat abruptly became a reality.

Light snow [was] obscuring most runway and taxiway markings. I approached the gate at a very slow pace (as the First Officer later described, "slower than a walk"). A Marshaller...was in place and had shovelled or plowed the lead-in line for us. The lead-in line was the only marking clearly visible on the ramp. There was no equipment adjacent to the Safety Zone, no hoses or cables in the Safety Zone, and...the jet bridge appeared to be in the correct location. We... verbalized that the safety zone was clear and I turned on to the lead-in line, continuing the very slow pace.

The snowfall had changed to very large flakes.... I checked the braking action and [announced that] braking was "good." Continuing down the lead-in line, I remained focused on the Marshaller with the snow falling. As we neared the jet bridge...I secured the number 2 engine and verbalized doing so.... Shortly thereafter, we felt a slight thump and the aircraft stopped. I did not notice any jet bridge movement and the Marshaller was still signalling forward taxi.

Something did not seem right. I set the parking brake and opened my sliding window.... As soon as I saw the proximity of the jet bridge to the number 1 engine, I immediately shut down the engine. I then scanned the instruments for any signs of FOD ingestion. All indications were normal. The Marshaller never seemed to realize that we contacted the jet bridge.... There was about an eight by three inch puncture in the top leading edge of the engine inlet.... I realize now that the jet bridge was angled out of the Safety Zone normally but then [had been] extended...into the Safety Zone.

NOTES:

DISTRACTION DURING THE DEPARTURE PROCESS

CHIRP

Aug 2017, Issue 123

The issue of servicing Flight Crew Bunks is not new. Recently I was operating on a flight and the 'heavy' captain had exactly the same problems that I remember from years past: ground staff failing to supply the agreed quantity of bedding. From my observation this happens on just about every 4-pilot departure - predictable and very sad. The 'heavy' captain was new to the fleet and didn't know the rules; I had the rules 'screen shot' on my iPad, which is why I got involved. I actually think that it is quite funny that a company like ours allows this to go on in a safety related industry. I suspect that CHIRP has bigger fish to fry than this but I also suspect that this is an industry-wide issue that takes various forms in different companies, which is why I've decided to share this little frustration with you. I know that it is an old model, but the Swiss cheese model still applies.

Lessons Learned:

Treat such minor issues as light entertainment!

CHIRP Comment: Distraction is a serious safety issue and the reporter is correct to encourage colleagues to try to rise above such irritations. But the irritation should not be there in the first place. Bedding is simply another element of the paraphernalia that is required for extended range operations. It should not be necessary for flight crew to bring sleeping bags to facilitate the rest they require in flight.

The operator has advised that it is aware of a number of issues on bedding provision at present, due in the main to two factors. It had been seeking to agree a common provision for different aircraft types as it currently had different agreements based upon aircraft type. In addition, the operator had changed provider and there were a few teething problems. The operator was attempting to improve the reliability of the provision but with many flights and destinations, different fleet agreements and a new supplier, it was taking some time.

NOTES:

MUSCLE MEMORY INTRODUCTION

CALLBACK

Muscle memory is an interesting physiological phenomenon involving our muscles and their interaction with the brain. The more often we perform a given physical action, the more likely we are to do it as needed, when needed, without having to think about the specific combination of movements involved. These habits thus become an unconscious process that occurs when triggered by a given circumstance or set of cues.

Practicing a procedure until the process is automatic develops muscle memory that can be crucial when an immediate action emergency (such as an engine failure at V_1) occurs. However, as in the incident reports below, muscle memory can be a problem when the cues are right, but the circumstances are wrong. That is when the brain has to be "conscious" enough to stop the automatic response of well-trained muscles.

The following reports recount a series of ground incidents in which muscle memory took over at the wrong time.

TAXI OUT, TOW BACK - B737

CALLBACK

Issue 434, March 2016

Faced with a distraction and a familiar set of circumstances, a B737 Captain let muscle memory take over just long enough to create an embarrassing situation.

Inoperative APU; second flight of the day; started the number one engine at the gate...; asked for taxi to a remote area for cross-bleed start of the number two engine. Stopping at the designated location, the aircraft began to shimmy slightly under braking. I stopped braking then applied brakes again. The shimmy did not happen again so I set the parking brake. I then grabbed the number one engine start lever and began to shut the number one engine down. Realizing what I was doing, I quickly returned it to the previous position, but the engine had already shut down. We were now on battery power. I told the Flight Attendants to remain seated, then told ATC we would need a tow back to the gate and we had one radio and would need to go off frequency to coordinate with Company Operations. We turned IRS 1 and 2 off and tried to explain to the passengers what had happened. We were back at the gate in approximately 10 minutes. We started the engine and did the procedure properly the second time. The remainder of the flight was uneventful.

I guess I would say it was muscle memory, the same motion as arriving at a gate, number two engine shut down, parking brake set. I should be more deliberate in all of my actions, but it happened so fast that the First Officer did not even have time to react. The brake shimmy was a distraction, but that does not excuse me from my action.

NOTES:

A BAD MATCH UP - B737

CALLBACK

Issue 434, March 2016

This B737 Captain's method of checking the start lever position was problem enough, but then muscle memory kicked in and made the situation worse.

It was my leg. Preflight activities had been normal and we were not rushed at all.... We had been instructed to hold short of [the runway] and were almost stopped. I had already called for the Before Takeoff Checklist and the First Officer challenged me with "Start Levers" at the next to last step in that checklist. I reached down to confirm "Idle." My practice has been to hold the start levers with my thumb and forefinger, confirm the idle detent position with a slight nudge forward and a slight nudge rearward, then to respond, "Idle." However this time with the slight nudge to the rear, the number one start lever felt like it was not quite fully down in the idle detent. It came up over the edge and I unintentionally shut down the number one engine. I was surprised and stunned.

I announced the situation to the First Officer and set the parking brake. Then instinctively I reached down again to confirm the start lever positions. At that point muscle memory kicked in and I must have "matched" the start lever heights. To my horror, when I nudged the levers rearward again, I unintentionally shut down the number two engine as well. I started the APU and put electrical power back on the aircraft. We told ATC that we had a problem and that it would be a few minutes before we could move. Feeling completely inept and embarrassed, I told the First Officer that we would start over and re-accomplish everything beginning with the Before Start Checklist. The First Officer agreed.

I made a short and embarrassing announcement to the Passengers and apologized for the delay while we dealt with a cockpit issue. We then flew an otherwise uneventful flight.

Several suggestions come to mind in order to prevent this from happening again. Primarily, I have changed the way that I check the start levers in the idle detent. No longer will I hold them with my thumb and forefinger. And no longer will I nudge them rearward, but only forward and down.

NOTES:

HOUSTON, WE HAVE AN ISSUE -
B737-800

CALLBACK

Issue 434, March 2016

A B737-800 Captain's prescription for inhibiting muscle memory involves slowing down and thinking before a particular situation triggers your internal automation and results in a dose of humility.

We were told to line up and wait. I brought the aircraft to a stop and, for some strange reason, I reached over and shut down both engines instead of setting the parking brake. We told Tower that we had an "issue" and would be in place for a minute or two and then we would have to taxi clear. We started the right engine and taxied clear of the runway so we could redo checklists and regroup. When the Tower later asked what our issue was, I think we told them that we had to look at a light. Actually, lots of lights.

With the start levers being right next to the parking brake, I guess that once my hand was on the start levers, positioned right next to the parking brake, muscle memory took over and moved them to off. I need to slow down and think about what I am doing before moving any switch or lever. This was definitely the healthiest dose of humility ever in my many years of flying.

NOTES:

THE BEST LAID PLANS - CRJ200

CALLBACK

Issue 434, March 2016

Even when the need for a non-standard sequence of events is recognized and planned for in advance, strong muscle memory concerning the standard sequence can prevail. This CRJ200 First Officer confirms that slowing down is the best way to engage the brain and disengage muscle memory.

When we received the aircraft, the previous crew had written up the #2 AC Generator. Maintenance came and deferred the generator. Per the MEL operations instructions, we were to keep the APU running for the entire flight. The Captain and I discussed this as part of our pre-departure briefing. When Tower cleared us to line up and wait, I ran the Takeoff Checklist and turned off the APU out of habit. I realized my mistake and informed the Captain. We notified the Tower that we would need to exit the runway and get back in line to restart the APU.

This incident illustrates why it is important to slow down when completing checklists and flows during abnormal operations to ensure they are completed properly. I shutdown the APU due to "muscle memory" during the Takeoff Checklist even though we had discussed the MEL procedures for the deferred AC Generator during the pre-departure briefing.

NOTES:

ROLLING IN THE SNOW - CRJ900

CALLBACK

Issue 434, March 2016

A CRJ900 Captain, faced with an oncoming snow plow, went for the brakes and engine reverse, but muscle memory had other ideas.

After landing, we were taxiing to our gate. The taxiways were snow covered with fair braking action. We had shut down our right engine and left the APU shut down. A snow plow was on our right and just ahead of us. I was watching him when he abruptly started to turn left into us. I applied the brakes, with minimal effectiveness, and I was going to apply reverse thrust, but muscle memory kicked in and I mistakenly shut down the left engine. We lost all power and rolled to a stop. The plow never completed his turn, but saw us and turned away. We informed ATC and started the APU to restart an engine. Within two minutes the engine was running again and we taxied to the gate without incident.

NOTES:

ARMED AND DANGEROUS - A320

CALLBACK

Issue 434, March 2016

An A320 First Officer got a first-hand lesson in how a busy, rushed environment can cause muscle memory to override a more methodical thought process.

This incident started about 5-10 minutes after the last passenger deplaned. Doors 1L and 2L were both open. There were many cleaners on the aircraft from the front to the back. The situation was busy at best, frantic at worst. I was standing on the front air stairs when a Flight Attendant asked me if I could supervise the opening of Door 2R. The cleaners were beating on the door to have it opened so that the trash could be emptied. I agreed to supervise since no other crew members were available. I followed the Flight Attendant to the back of the airplane where various ramp personnel were in the aft galley conducting their work. The Flight Attendant proceeded to arm the door as it had been disarmed from deplaning. It was at this point that I became confused. Before I could intervene, the Flight Attendant pulled up on the handle. The door opened and the slide blew. Luckily, no one was injured.

I should have done a better job confirming what was actually going on and tried to slow the process down.... The overall issue for me was being distracted, rushed and uncertain of my supervision objective. I also believe the Flight Attendant was trying to do the right thing, especially as a new employee. She was rushed and getting pressure from the cleaners. In retrospect, I think she was operating on muscle memory. Since she had already disarmed the door, the next event was to arm it.

NOTES:

CHAPTER 9

AVIATION QUOTES

"Clearly this was an out of the ordinary landing, but I was just doing my job and any one of our pilots would have taken the same actions."
Captain David Williams
Virgin Atlantic flight 43
He safely landed his B747 at London Gatwick with 447 people on board with no starboard outer main landing gear. BBC News, 31 December 2014

"This man deserves a medal as big as a frying pan. He has done a fantastic job."
Unnamed airport worker regards Captain Peter Burkill, British Airways B-777 pilot, following safe crash-landing at Heathrow Airport, 17 January 2008

"There's simply no substitute for experience in terms of aviation safety."
Captain Chesley B. 'Sully' Sullenberger

"I have long been on record that I believe our probable cause findings are primarily a vehicle for affecting positive changes, and not for placing blame. In accident investigation and prevention efforts, I don't believe that we are constrained to a narrow construct of causality."

John K. Lauber

NTSB Board Report of an April 2, 1992, CFIT accident in Hawaii, published in 1993.

"I learned that danger is relative, and the inexperience can be a magnifying glass."

Charles A. Lindbergh

"Challenger was lost because NASA came to believe its own propaganda. The agency's deeply impacted cultural hubris had it that technology — engineering — would always triumph over random disaster if certain rules were followed. The engineers-turned-technocrats could not bring themselves to accept the psychology of machines with abandoning the core principle of their own faith: equations, geometry, and repetition — physical law, precision design, and testing — must defy chaos. No matter that astronauts and cosmonauts had perished in precisely designed and carefully tested machines. Solid engineering could always provide a safety margin, because the engineers believed, there was complete safety in numbers."

William E. Burrows, This New Ocean, 1998

"The warm Hawaiian sun was blaring in as we went

eastbound. I just closed my eyes for a minute, enjoying the sunshine and dozed off."

Scott Oltman, captain of go! flight 1002 on 13 February 2007, who along with the first officer fell asleep heading out over the ocean during an inter-island flight. They awoke in time to fly back to land. From a subsequent NTSB interview.

GLOSSARY

ICAO ABBREVIATIONS AND CODES

A

A Amber

AAA (or AAB, AAC . . . etc., in sequence) Amended meteorological message(message type designator)

A/A Air-to-air

AAD Assigned altitude deviation

AAIM Aircraft autonomous integrity monitoring

AAL Above aerodrome level

ABI Advance boundary information

ABM Abeam

ABN Aerodrome beacon

ABT About

ABV Above

AC Altocumulus

ACARS† (to be pronounced "AY-CARS") Aircraft communication addressing and reporting system

ACAS† Airborne collision avoidance system

ACC‡ Area control centre or area control

ACCID Notification of an aircraft accident

ACFT Aircraft

ACK Acknowledge

ACL Altimeter check location

ACN Aircraft classification number

ACP Acceptance (message type designator)

ACPT Accept or accepted

ACT Active or activated or activity

AD Aerodrome

ADA Advisory area

ADC Aerodrome chart

ADDN Addition or additional

ADF‡ Automatic direction-finding equipment

ADIZ† (to be pronounced "AY-DIZ") Air defence identification zone

ADJ Adjacent

ADO Aerodrome office (specify service)

ADR Advisory route

ADS* The address (when this abbreviation is used to request a repetition, the question mark (IMI) precedes the abbreviation, e.g. IMI ADS) (to be used in AFS as a procedure signal) A

ALERFA† Alert phase

ALR Alerting (message type designator)

ALRS Alerting service

ALS Approach lighting system

ALT Altitude

ALTN Alternate or alternating (light alternates in colour)

ALTN Alternate (aerodrome)

AMA Area minimum altitude

AMD Amend or amended (used to indicate amended meteorological message; message type designator)

AMDT Amendment (AIP Amendment)

AMS Aeronautical mobile service

AMSL Above mean sea level

AMSS Aeronautical mobile satellite service

ANC . . . Aeronautical chart — 1:500 000 (followed by name/title)

ANCS . . . Aeronautical navigation chart — small scale (followed by name/title and scale)

ANS Answer

AOC . . . Aerodrome obstacle chart (followed by type and name/title)

AP Airport

APAPI † (to be pronounced "AY-PAPI") Abbreviated precision approach path indicator

APCH Approach

APDC . . . Aircraft parking/docking chart (followed by name/title)

APN Apron

APP Approach control office or approach control or approach control service

APR April

APRX Approximate or approximately

APSG After passing

APV Approve or approved or approval

ARC Area chart

ARNG Arrange

ARO Air traffic services reporting office

ARP Aerodrome reference point

ARP Air-report (message type designator)

ARQ Automatic error correction

ARR Arrival (message type designator)

ARR Arrive or arrival

ARS Special air-report (message type designator)

ARST Arresting (specify (part of) aircraft arresting equipment)

AS Altostratus

ASC Ascend to or ascending to

ASDA Accelerate-stop distance available

ASE Altimetry system error

ASHTAM Special series NOTAM notifying, by means of a specific format, change in activity of a volcano, a volcanic eruption and/or volcanic ash cloud that is of significance to aircraft operations

ASPH Asphalt

AT . . . At (followed by time at which weather change is forecast to occur)

ATA‡ Actual time of arrival

ATC‡ Air traffic control (in general)

ATCSMAC. . . Air traffic control surveillance minimum altitude chart (followed by name/title)

ATD‡ Actual time of departure

ATFM Air traffic flow management

ATIS† Automatic terminal information service

ATM Air traffic management

ATN Aeronautical telecommunication network

ATP . . . At . . . (time or place)

ATS Air traffic services

ATTN Attention

AT-VASIS† (to be pronounced "AY-TEE-VASIS") Abbreviated T visual approach slope indicator system

ATZ Aerodrome traffic zone

AUG August

AUTH Authorized or authorization

AUW All up weight

AUX Auxiliary

AVBL Available or availability

AVG Average

AVGAS† Aviation gasoline

AWTA Advise at what time able

AWY Airway

AZM Azimuth

B

B Blue

BA Braking action

BARO-VNAV† (to be pronounced "BAA-RO-VEENAV") Barometric vertical navigation

BASE† Cloud base

BCFG Fog patches

BCN Beacon (aeronautical ground light)

BCST Broadcast

BDRY Boundary

BECMG Becoming

BFR Before

BKN Broken

BL . . . Blowing (followed by DU = dust, SA = sand or SN = snow)

BLDG Building

BLO Below clouds

BLW ... Below ...

BOMB Bombing

BR Mist

BRF Short (used to indicate the type of approach desired or required)

BRG Bearing

BRKG Braking

BS Commercial broadcasting station

BTL Between layers

BTN Between

BUFR Binary universal form for the representation of meteorological data

C

... C Centre (preceded by runway designation number to identify a parallel runway)

C Degrees Celsius (Centigrade)

CA Course to an altitude

CAT Category

CAT Clear air turbulence

CAVOK† (to be pronounced "KAV-OH-KAY") Visibility, cloud and present weather better than prescribed values or conditions

CB‡ (to be pronounced "CEE BEE") Cumulonimbus

CC Cirrocumulus

CCA (or CCB, CCC . . . etc., in sequence) Corrected meteorological message (message type designator)

CD Candela

CDN Coordination (message type designator)

CF Change frequency to . . .

CF Course to a fix

CFM* Confirm or I confirm (to be used in AFS as a procedure signal)

CGL Circling guidance light(s)

CH Channel

CH# This is a channel-continuity-check of transmission to permit comparison of your record of channel sequence numbers of messages received on the channel (to be used in AFS as a procedure signal)

CHEM Chemical

CHG Modification (message type designator)

CI Cirrus

CIDIN† Common ICAO data interchange network

CIT Near or over large towns

CIV Civil

CK Check

CL Centre line

CLA Clear type of ice formation

CLBR Calibration

CLD Cloud

CLG Calling

CLIMB-OUT Climb-out area

CLR Clear(s) or cleared to . . . or clearance

CLRD Runway(s) cleared (used in METAR/SPECI)

CLSD Close or closed or closing
CM Centimetre
CMB Climb to or climbing to
CMPL Completion or completed or complete
CNL Cancel or cancelled
CNL Flight plan cancellation (message type designator)
CNS Communications, navigation and surveillance
COM Communications
CONC Concrete
COND Condition
CONS Continuous
CONST Construction or constructed
CONT Continue(s) or continued
COOR Coordinate or coordination
COORD Coordinates
COP Change-over point
COR Correct or correction or corrected (used to indicate corrected meteorological message; message type designator)
COT At the coast
COV Cover or covered or covering
CPDLC‡ Controller-pilot data link communications
CPL Current flight plan (message type designator)
CRC Cyclic redundancy check
CRM Collision risk model
CRZ Cruise
CS Call sign
CS Cirrostratus
CTA Control area
CTAM Climb to and maintain
CTC Contact
CTL Control
CTN Caution
CTR Control zone
CU Cumulus

CUF Cumuliform
CUST Customs
CVR Cockpit voice recorder
CW Continuous wave
CWY Clearway

D

D Downward (tendency in RVR during previous 10 minutes)
D . . . Danger area (followed by identification)
DA Decision altitude
D-ATIS† (to be pronounced "DEE-ATIS") Data link automatic terminal information service
DCD Double channel duplex
DCKG Docking
DCP Datum crossing point
DCPC Direct controller-pilot communications
DCS Double channel simplex
DCT Direct (in relation to flight plan clearances and type of approach)
DE* From (used to precede the call sign of the calling station) (to be used in AFS as a procedure signal)
DEC December
DEG Degrees
DEP Depart or departure
DEP Departure (message type designator)
DEPO Deposition
DER Departure end of the runway
DES Descend to or descending to
DEST Destination
DETRESFA† Distress phase
DEV Deviation or deviating
DF Direction finding
DFDR Digital flight data recorder
DFTI Distance from touchdown indicator

DH Decision height

DIF Diffuse

DIST Distance

DIV Divert or diverting

DLA Delay or delayed

DLA Delay (message type designator)

DLIC Data link initiation capability

DLY Daily

DME‡ Distance measuring equipment

DNG Danger or dangerous

DOM Domestic

DP Dew point temperature

DPT Depth

DR Dead reckoning

DR . . . Low drifting (followed by DU = dust, SA = sand or SN = snow)

DRG During

DS Dust-storm

DSB Double sideband

DTAM Descend to and maintain

DTG Date-time group

DTHR Displaced runway threshold

DTRT Deteriorate or deteriorating

DTW Dual tandem wheels

DU Dust

DUC Dense upper cloud

DUPE# This is a duplicate message (to be used in AFS as a procedure signal)

DUR Duration

D-VOLMET Data link VOLMET

DVOR Doppler VOR

DW Dual wheels

DZ Drizzle

E

E East or eastern longitude

EATExpected approach time

EB Eastbound

EDA Elevation differential area

EEE# Error (to be used in AFS as a procedure signal)

EET Estimated elapsed time

EFC Expect further clearance

EFIS† (to be pronounced "EE-FIS") Electronic flight instrument system

EGNOS † (to be pronounced "EGG-NOS") European geostationary navigation overlay service

EHF Extremely high frequency [30 000 to 300 000 MHz]

ELBA† Emergency location beacon — aircraft

ELEV Elevation

ELR Extra long range

ELT Emergency locator transmitter

EM Emission

EMBD Embedded in a layer (to indicate cumulonimbus embedded in layers of other clouds)

EMERG Emergency

END Stop-end (related to RVR)

ENE East-north-east

ENG Engine

ENR En route

ENRC . . . Enroute chart (followed by name/title)

EOBT Estimated off-block time

EQPT Equipment

ER* Here . . . or herewith

ESE East-south-east

EST Estimate or estimated or estimation (message type designator)

ETA*‡ Estimated time of arrival or estimating arrival

ETD‡ Estimated time of departure or estimating departure

ETO Estimated time over significant point
EUR RODEX European regional OPMET data exchange
EV Every
EVS Enhanced vision system
EXC Except
EXER Exercises or exercising or to exercise
EXP Expect or expected or expecting
EXTD Extend or extending

F

F Fixed
FA Course from a fix to an altitude
FAC Facilities
FAF Final approach fix
FAL Facilitation of international air transport
FAP Final approach point
FAS Final approach segment
FATO Final approach and take-off area
FAX Facsimile transmission
FBL Light (used to indicate the intensity of weather phenomena, interference or static reports, e.g. FBL RA = light rain)
FC Funnel cloud (tornado or water spout)
FCST Forecast
FCT Friction coefficient
FDPS Flight data processing system
FEB February
FEW Few
FG Fog
FIC Flight information centre
FIR‡ Flight information region
FIS Flight information service
FISA Automated flight information service
FL Flight level
FLD Field

FLG Flashing

FLR Flares

FLT Flight

FLTCK Flight check

FLUC Fluctuating or fluctuation or fluctuated

FLW Follow(s) or following

FLY Fly or flying

FM Course from a fix to manual termination (used in navigation database coding)

FM From

FM . . . From (followed by time weather change is forecast to begin)

FMC Flight management computer

FMS‡ Flight management system

FMU Flow management unit

FNA Final approach

FPAP Flight path alignment point

FPL Filed flight plan (message type designator)

FPM Feet per minute

FPR Flight plan route

FR Fuel remaining

FREQ Frequency

FRI Friday

FRNG Firing

FRONT† Front (relating to weather)

FROST† Frost (used in aerodrome warnings)

FRQ Frequent

FSL Full stop landing

FSS Flight service station

FST First

FT Feet (dimensional unit)

FTE Flight technical error

FTP Fictitious threshold point

FTT Flight technical tolerance

FU Smoke

FZ Freezing

FZDZ Freezing drizzle

FZFG Freezing fog

FZRA Freezing rain

G

G Green

G . . . Variations from the mean wind speed (gusts) (followed by figures in METAR/SPECI and TAF)

GA Go ahead, resume sending (to be used in AFS as a procedure signal)

G/A Ground-to-air

G/A/G Ground-to-air and air-to-ground

GAGAN † GPS and geostationary earth orbit augmented navigation

GAIN Airspeed or headwind gain

GAMET Area forecast for low-level flights

GARP GBAS azimuth reference point

GBAS† (to be pronounced "GEE-BAS") Ground-based augmentation system

GCA‡ Ground controlled approach system or ground controlled approach

GEN General

GEO Geographic or true

GES Ground earth station

GLD Glider

GLONASS† (to be pronounced "GLO-NAS") Global orbiting navigation satellite system

GLS‡ GBAS landing system

GMC . . . Ground movement chart (followed by name/title)

GND Ground

GNDCK Ground check

GNSS‡ Global navigation satellite system

GP Glide path

GPA Glide path angle

GPIP Glide path intercept point

GPS‡ Global positioning system

GPWS‡ Ground proximity warning system

GR Hail

GRAS† (to be pronounced "GRASS") Ground-based regional augmentation system

GRASS Grass landing area

GRIB Processed meteorological data in the form of grid point values expressed in binary form (meteorological code)

GRVL Gravel

GS Ground speed

GS Small hail and/or snow pellets

GUND Geoid undulation

H

H High pressure area or the centre of high pressure

H24 Continuous day and night service

HA Holding/racetrack to an altitude

HAPI Helicopter approach path indicator

HBN Hazard beacon

HDF High frequency direction-finding station

HDG Heading

HEL Helicopter

HF‡ High frequency [3 000 to 30 000 kHz]

HF Holding/racetrack to a fix

HGT Height or height above

HJ Sunrise to sunset

HLDG Holding

HM Holding/racetrack to a manual termination

HN Sunset to sunrise

HO Service available to meet operational requirements

HOL Holiday

HOSP Hospital aircraft

HPA Hectopascal

HR Hours

HS Service available during hours of scheduled operations

HUD Head-up display

HURCN Hurricane

HVDF High and very high frequency direction finding stations (at the same location)

HVY Heavy

HVY Heavy (used to indicate the intensity of weather phenomena, e.g. HVY RA = heavy rain)

HX No specific working hours

HYR Higher

HZ Haze

HZ Hertz (cycle per second)

I

IAC ... Instrument approach chart (followed by name/title)

IAF Initial approach fix

IAO In and out of clouds

IAP Instrument approach procedure

IARIntersection of air routes

IAS Indicated airspeed

IBN Identification beacon

IC Ice crystals (very small ice crystals in suspension, also known as diamond dust)

ICE Icing

ID Identifier or identify

IDENT† Identification

IF Intermediate approach fix

IFF Identification friend/foe

IFR‡ Instrument flight rules

IGA International general aviation

ILS‡ Instrument landing system

IM Inner marker
IMC‡ Instrument meteorological conditions
IMG Immigration
IMI* Interrogation sign (question mark) (to be used in AFS as a procedure signal)
IMPR Improve or improving
IMT Immediate or immediately
INA Initial approach
INBD Inbound
INC In cloud
INCERFA† Uncertainty phase
INFO† Information
INOP Inoperative
INP If not possible
INPR In progress
INS Inertial navigation system
INSTL Install or installed or installation
INSTR Instrument
INT Intersection
INTL International
INTRG Interrogator
INTRP Interrupt or interruption or interrupted
INTSF Intensify or intensifying
INTST Intensity
IR Ice on runway
IRS Inertial reference system
ISA International standard atmosphere
ISB Independent sideband
ISOL Isolated

J

JAN January
JTST Jet stream
JUL July

JUN June

K

KG Kilograms
KHZ Kilohertz
KIAS Knots indicated airspeed
KM Kilometres
KMH Kilometres per hour
KPA Kilopascal
KT Knots
KW Kilowatts

L

... L Left (preceded by runway designation number to identify a parallel runway)
L Locator (see LM, LO)
L Low pressure area or the centre of low pressure
LAM Logical acknowledgement (message type designator)
LAN Inland
LAT Latitude
LCA Local or locally or location or located
LDA Landing distance available
LDAH Landing distance available, helicopter
LDG Landing
LDI Landing direction indicator
LEN Length
LF Low frequency [30 to 300 kHz]
LGT Light or lighting
LGTD Lighted
LIH Light intensity high
LIL Light intensity low
LIM Light intensity medium
LINE Line (used in SIGMET)
LM Locator, middle

LMT Local mean time

LNAV† (to be pronounced "EL-NAV") Lateral navigation

LNG Long (used to indicate the type of approach desired or required)

LO Locator, outer

LOC Localizer

LONG Longitude

LORAN† LORAN (long range air navigation system)

LOSS Airspeed or headwind loss

LPV Localizer performance with vertical guidance

LR The last message received by me was . . . (to be used in AFS as a procedure signal)

LRG Long range

LS The last message sent by me was . . . or Last message was . . . (to be used in AFS as a procedure signal)

LTD Limited

LTP Landing threshold point

LTT Landline teletypewriter

LV Light and variable (relating to wind)

LVE Leave or leaving

LVL Level

LVP Low visibility procedures

LYR Layer or layered

M

. . . M Metres (preceded by figures)

M . . . Mach number (followed by figures)

M . . . Minimum value of runway visual range (followed by figures in METAR/SPECI)

MAA Maximum authorized altitude

MAG Magnetic

MAHF Missed approach holding fix

MAINT Maintenance

MAP Aeronautical maps and charts

MAPT Missed approach point

MAR At sea

MAR March

MAS Manual Al simplex

MATF Missed approach turning fix

MAX Maximum

MAY May

MBST Microburst

MCA Minimum crossing altitude

MCW Modulated continuous wave

MDA Minimum descent altitude

MDF Medium frequency direction-finding station

MDH Minimum descent height

MEA Minimum en-route altitude

MEHT Minimum eye height over threshold (for visual approach slope indicator systems)

MET† Meteorological or meteorology

METAR† Aerodrome routine meteorological report (in meteorological code)

MET REPORT Local routine meteorological report (in abbreviated plain language)

MF Medium frequency [300 to 3 000 kHz]

MHDF Medium and high frequency direction finding stations (at the same location)

MHVDF Medium, high and very high frequency direction-finding stations (at the same location)

MHZ Megahertz

MID Mid-point (related to RVR)

MIFG Shallow fog

MIL Military

MIN* Minutes

MIS Missing . . . (transmission identification) (to be used in AFS as a procedure signal)

MKR Marker radio beacon

MLS‡ Microwave landing system

MM Middle marker

MNM Minimum

MNPS Minimum navigation performance specifications

MNT Monitor or monitoring or monitored

MNTN Maintain

MOA Military operating area

MOC Minimum obstacle clearance (required)

MOCA Minimum obstacle clearance altitude

MOD Moderate (used to indicate the intensity of weather phenomena, interference or static reports, e.g. MODRA = moderate rain)

MON Above mountains

MON Monday

MOPS† Minimum operational performance standards

MOV Move or moving or movement

MPS Metres per second

MRA Minimum reception altitude

MRG Medium range

MRP ATS/MET reporting point

MS Minus

MSA Minimum sector altitude

MSAS † (to be pronounced "EM-SAS") Multifunctional transport satellite (MTSAT) satellite-based augmentation system

MSAW Minimum safe altitude warning

MSG Message

MSL Mean sea level

MSR# Message . . . (transmission identification) has been misrouted (to be used in AFS as a procedure signal)

MSSR Monopulse secondary surveillance radar

MT Mountain

MTU Metric units

MTW Mountain waves

MVDF Medium and very high frequency direction- finding stations (at the same location)

MWO Meteorological watch office

MX Mixed type of ice formation (white and clear)

N

N No distinct tendency (in RVR during previous 10 minutes)

N North or northern latitude

NADP Noise abatement departure procedure

NASC† National AIS system centre

NAT North Atlantic

NAV Navigation

NB Northbound

NBFR Not before

NC No change

NCD No cloud detected (used in automated METAR/SPECI)

NDB‡ Non-directional radio beacon

NDV No directional variations available (used in automated METAR/SPECI)

NE North-east

NEB North-eastbound

NEG No or negative or permission not granted or that is not correct

NGT Night

NIL*† None or I have nothing to send to you

NM Nautical miles

NML Normal

NN No name, unnamed

NNE North-north-east

NNW North-north-west

NO No (negative) (to be used in AFS as a procedure signal)

NOF International NOTAM office

NOSIG † No significant change (used in trend-type landing forecasts)

NOTAM† A notice distributed by means of telecommunication containing information concerning the establishment, condition or change in any aeronautical facility, service, procedure or hazard, the timely knowledge of which is essential to personnel concerned with flight operations

NOV November

NOZ‡ Normal operating zone

NPA Non-precision approach

NR Number

NRH No reply heard

NS Nimbostratus

NSC Nil significant cloud

NSE Navigation system error

NSW Nil significant weather

NTL National

NTZ‡ No transgression zone

NW North-west

NWB North-westbound

NXT Next

O

OAC Oceanic area control centre

OAS Obstacle assessment surface

OBS Observe or observed or observation

OBSC Obscure or obscured or obscuring

OBST Obstacle

OCA Obstacle clearance altitude

OCA Oceanic control area

OCC Occulting (light)

OCH Obstacle clearance height

OCNL Occasional or occasionally

OCS Obstacle clearance surface

OCT October

OFZ Obstacle free zone

OGN Originate (to be used in AFS as a procedure signal)

OHD Overhead

OIS Obstacle identification surface

OK* We agree or It is correct (to be used in AFS as a procedure signal)

OLDI† On-line data interchange

OM Outer marker

OPA Opaque, white type of ice formation

OPC Control indicated is operational control

OPMET† Operational meteorological (information)

OPN Open or opening or opened

OPR Operator or operate or operative or operating or operational

OPS† Operations

O/R On request

ORD Order

OSV Ocean station vessel

OTP On top

OTS Organized track system

OUBD Outbound

OVC Overcast

P

P . . . Maximum value of wind speed or runway visual range (followed by figures in METAR/SPECI and TAF)

P . . . Prohibited area (followed by identification)

PA Precision approach

PALS Precision approach lighting system (specify category)

PANS Procedures for air navigation services

PAPI† Precision approach path indicator

PAR‡ Precision approach radar

PARL Parallel

PATC . . . Precision approach terrain chart (followed by name/title)

PAX Passenger(s)

PBN Performance-based navigation

PCD Proceed or proceeding

PCL Pilot-controlled lighting

PCN Pavement classification number

PDC‡ Pre-departure clearance

PDG Procedure design gradient

PER Performance

PERM Permanent

PIB Pre-flight information bulletin

PJE Parachute jumping exercise

PL Ice pellets

PLA Practice low approach

PLN Flight plan

PLVL Present level

PN Prior notice required

PNR Point of no return

PO Dust/sand whirls (dust devils)

POB Persons on board

POSS Possible

PPI Plan position indicator

PPR Prior permission required

PPSN Present position

PRFG Aerodrome partially covered by fog

PRI Primary

PRKG Parking

PROB† Probability

PROC Procedure

PROV Provisional

PRP Point-in-space reference point

PS Plus

PSG Passing

PSN Position
PSP Pierced steel plank
PSR‡ Primary surveillance radar
PSYS Pressure system(s)
PTN Procedure turn
PTS Polar track structure
PWR Power

Q

QD Do you intend to ask me for a series of bearings? or I intend to ask you for a series of bearings (to be used in radiotelegraphy as a Q Code)

QDM‡ Magnetic heading (zero wind)

QDR Magnetic bearing

QFE ‡ Atmospheric pressure at aerodrome elevation (or at runway threshold)

QFU Magnetic orientation of runway

QGE What is my distance to your station? or Your distance to my station is (distance figures and units) (to be used in radiotelegraphy as a Q Code)

QJH Shall I run my test tape/a test sentence? or Run your test tape/a test sentence (to
be used in AFS as a Q Code)

QNH‡ Altimeter sub-scale setting to obtain elevation when on the ground

QSP Will you relay to . . . free of charge? or I will relay to . . . free of charge (to be used in AFS as a Q Code)

QTA Shall I cancel telegram number . . .? or Cancel telegram number . . . (to be used in AFS as a Q Code)

QTE True bearing

QTF Will you give me the position of my station according to the bearings taken by the D/F stations which you control? or The position of your station according to the bearings taken by the D/F stations that I control was . . . latitude . . . longitude (or other indication of position), class . . . at . . . hours (to be used in radiotelegraphy as a Q Code)

QUAD Quadrant

QUJ Will you indicate the TRUE track to reach you? or The TRUE track to reach me is . . . degrees at . . . hours (to be used in radiotelegraphy as a Q Code)

R

. . . R Right (preceded by runway designation number to identify a parallel runway)

R Rate of turn

R Red

R . . . Restricted area (followed by identification)

R . . . Runway (followed by figures in METAR/SPECI)

R* Received (acknowledgement of receipt) (to be used in AFS as a procedure signal)

RA Rain

RA Resolution advisory

RAC Rules of the air and air traffic services

RAG Ragged

RAG Runway arresting gear

RAI Runway alignment indicator

RAIM† Receiver autonomous integrity monitoring

RASC† Regional AIS system centre

RASS Remote altimeter setting source

RB Rescue boat

RCA Reach cruising altitude

RCC Rescue coordination centre

RCF Radio-communication failure (message type designator)

RCH Reach or reaching

RCL Runway centre line

RCLL Runway centre line light(s)

RCLR Recleared

RCP‡ Required communication performance

RDH Reference datum height

RDL Radial

RDO Radio

RE Recent (used to qualify weather phenomena, e.g. RERA = recent rain)

REC Receive or receiver

REDL Runway edge light(s)

REF Reference to . . . or refer to . . .

REG Registration

RENL Runway end light(s)

REP Report or reporting or reporting point

REQ Request or requested

RERTE Re-route

RESA Runway end safety area

RF Constant radius arc to a fix

RG Range (lights)

RHC Right-hand circuit

RIF Reclearance in flight

RIME† Rime (used in aerodrome warnings)

RITE Right (direction of turn)

RL Report leaving

RLA Relay to

RLCE Request level change en route

RLLS Runway lead-in lighting system

RLNA Request level not available

RMK Remark

RNAV† (to be pronounced "AR-NAV") Area navigation

RNG Radio range

RNP‡ Required navigation performance

ROBEX† Regional OPMET bulletin exchange (scheme)

ROC Rate of climb

ROD Rate of descent

RON Receiving only

RPDS Reference path data selector

RPI‡ Radar position indicator

RPL Repetitive flight plan

RPLC Replace or replaced

RPS Radar position symbol

RPT* Repeat or I repeat (to be used in AFS as a procedure signal)

RQ* Request (to be used in AFS as a procedure signal)

RQMNTS Requirements

RQP Request flight plan (message type designator)

RQS Request supplementary flight plan (message type designator)

RR Report reaching

RRA (or RRB, RRC . . . etc., in sequence) Delayed meteorological message (message type designator)

RSC Rescue sub-centre

RSCD Runway surface condition

RSP Responder beacon

RSR En-route surveillance radar

RSS Root sum square

RTD Delayed (used to indicate delayed meteorological message; message type designator)

RTE Route

RTF Radiotelephone

RTG Radiotelegraph

RTHL Runway threshold light(s)

RTN Return or returned or returning

RTODAH Rejected take-off distance available, helicopter

RTS Return to service

RTT Radio-teletypewriter

RTZL Runway touchdown zone light(s)

RUT Standard regional route transmitting frequencies

RV Rescue vessel

RVR‡ Runway visual range

RVSM‡ Reduced vertical separation minimum (300 m (1 000 ft)) between FL 290 and FL 410

RWY Runway

S

S South or southern latitude

S . . . State of the sea (followed by figures in METAR/SPECI)

SA Sand

SALS Simple approach lighting system

SAN Sanitary

SAP As soon as possible

SAR Search and rescue

SARPS Standards and Recommended Practices [ICAO]

SAT Saturday

SATCOM† Satellite communication

SB Southbound

SBAS† (to be pronounced "ESS-BAS") Satellite-based augmentation system

SC Stratocumulus

SCT Scattered

SD Standard deviation

SDBY Stand by

SDF Step down fix

SE South-east

SEA Sea (used in connection with sea-surface temperature and state of the sea)

SEB South-eastbound

SEC Seconds

SECN Section

SECT Sector

SELCAL† Selective calling system

SEP September

SER Service or servicing or served

SEV Severe (used e.g. to qualify icing and turbulence reports)

SFC Surface

SG Snow grains

SGL Signal

SH . . . Shower (followed by RA = rain, SN = snow, PL = ice pellets, GR = hail, GS

= small hail and/or snow pellets or combinations thereof, e.g. SHRASN = showers of rain and snow)

SHF Super high frequency [3 000 to 30 000 MHz]

SI International system of units

SID† Standard instrument departure

SIF Selective identification feature

SIG Significant

SIGMET † Information concerning en-route weather phenomena which may affect the safety of aircraft operations

SIMUL Simultaneous or simultaneously

SIWL Single isolated wheel load

SKED Schedule or scheduled

SLP Speed limiting point

SLW Slow

SMC Surface movement control

SMR Surface movement radar

SN Snow

SNOCLO Aerodrome closed due to snow (used in METAR/SPECI)

SNOWTAM† Special series NOTAM notifying the presence or removal of hazardous conditions due to snow, ice, slush or standing water associated with snow, slush and ice on the movement area, by means of a specific format

SOC Start of climb

SPECI† Aerodrome special meteorological report (in meteorological code)

SPECIAL† Local special meteorological report (in abbreviated plain language)

SPI Special position indicator

SPL Supplementary flight plan (message type designator)

SPOC SAR point of contact

SPOT† Spot wind

SQ Squall

SQL Squall line

SR Sunrise

SRA Surveillance radar approach

SRE Surveillance radar element of precision approach radar system

SRG Short range

SRR Search and rescue region

SRY Secondary

SS Sandstorm

SS Sunset

SSB Single sideband

SSE South-south-east

SSR‡ Secondary surveillance radar

SST Supersonic transport

SSW South-south-west

ST Stratus

STA Straight-in approach

STAR† Standard instrument arrival

STD Standard

STF Stratiform

STN Station

STNR Stationary

STOL Short take-off and landing

STS Status

STWL Stopway light(s)

SUBJ Subject to

SUN Sunday

SUP Supplement (AIP Supplement)

SUPPS Regional supplementary procedures

SVC Service message

SVCBL Serviceable
SW South-west
SWB South-westbound
SWY Stopway

T

T Temperature
. . . T True (preceded by a bearing to indicate reference to True North)
TA Traffic advisory
TA Transition altitude
TAA Terminal arrival altitude
TACAN† UHF tactical air navigation aid
TAF† Aerodrome forecast (in meteorological code)
TA/H Turn at an altitude/height
TAIL† Tail wind
TAR Terminal area surveillance radar
TAS True airspeed
TAX Taxiing or taxi
TC Tropical cyclone
TCAC Tropical cyclone advisory centre
TCAS RA † (to be pronounced "TEE-CAS-AR-AY") Traffic alert and collision avoidance system resolution advisory
TCH Threshold crossing height
TCU Towering cumulus
TDO Tornado
TDZ Touchdown zone
TECR Technical reason
TEL Telephone
TEMPO† Temporary or temporarily
TF Track to fix
TFC Traffic
TGL Touch-and-go landing
TGS Taxiing guidance system

THR Threshold
THRU Through
THU Thursday
TIBA† Traffic information broadcast by aircraft
TIL† Until
TIP Until past . . . (place)
TKOF Take-off
TL . . . Till (followed by time by which weather change is forecast to end)
TLOF Touchdown and lift-off area
TMA‡ Terminal control area
TN . . . Minimum temperature (followed by figures in TAF)
TNA Turn altitude
TNH Turn height
TO . . . To . . . (place)
TOC Top of climb
TODA Take-off distance available
TODAH Take-off distance available, helicopter
TOP† Cloud top
TORA Take-off run available
TOX Toxic
TP Turning point
TR Track
TRA Temporary reserved airspace
TRANS Transmits or transmitter
TREND† Trend forecast
TRL Transition level
TROP Tropopause
TS Thunderstorm (in aerodrome reports and forecasts, TS used alone means thunder heard but no precipitation at the aerodrome)
TS . . . Thunderstorm (followed by RA = rain, SN = snow, PL = ice pellets, GR = hail, GS = small hail and/or snow pellets or combinations thereof, e.g. TSRASN = thunderstorm with rain and snow)
TSUNAMI† Tsunami (used in aerodrome warnings)

TT Teletypewriter

TUE Tuesday

TURB Turbulence

T-VASIS† (to be pronounced "TEE-VASIS") T visual approach slope indicator system

TVOR Terminal VOR

TWR Aerodrome control tower or aerodrome control

TWY Taxiway

TWYL Taxiway-link

TX ... Maximum temperature (followed by figures in TAF)

TXT* Text (when the abbreviation is used to request a repetition, the question mark (IMI) precedes the abbreviation, e.g. IMI TXT) (to be used in AFS as a procedure signal)

TYP Type of aircraft

TYPH Typhoon

U

U Upward (tendency in RVR during previous 10 minutes)

UA Unmanned aircraft

UAB ... Until advised by ...

UAC Upper area control centre

UAR Upper air route

UAS Unmanned aircraft system

UDF Ultra high frequency direction-finding station

UFN Until further notice

UHDT Unable higher due traffic

UHF‡ Ultra high frequency [300 to 3 000 MHz]

UIC Upper information centre

UIR‡ Upper flight information region

ULR Ultra long range

UNA Unable

UNAP Unable to approve

UNL Unlimited

UNREL Unreliable

UP   Unidentified   precipitation   (used   in   automated METAR/SPECI)

U/S Unserviceable

UTA Upper control area

UTC‡ Coordinated Universal Time

V

... V ... Variations from the mean wind direction (preceded and followed by figures in METAR/SPECI, e.g. 350V070)

VA Heading to an altitude

VA Volcanic ash

VAAC Volcanic ash advisory centre

VAC ... Visual approach chart (followed by name/title)

VAL In valleys

VAN Runway control van

VAR Magnetic variation

VAR Visual-aural radio range

VASIS Visual approach slope indicator systems

VC ... Vicinity of the aerodrome (followed by FG = fog, FC = funnel cloud, SH = shower, PO = dust/sand whirls, BLDU = blowing dust, BLSA = blowing sand, BLSN = blowing snow, DS = dust-storm, SS = sandstorm, TS = thunderstorm or VA = volcanic ash, e.g. VCFG = vicinity fog)

VCY Vicinity

VDF Very high frequency direction-finding station

VER Vertical

VFR‡ Visual flight rules

VHF‡ Very high frequency [30 to 300 MHz]

VI Heading to an intercept

VIP‡ Very important person

VIS Visibility

VLF Very low frequency [3 to 30 kHz]

VLR Very long range

VM Heading to a manual termination

VMC‡ Visual meteorological conditions

VNAV† (to be pronounced "VEE-NAV") Vertical navigation

VOLMET† Meteorological information for aircraft in flight

VOR‡ VHF omnidirectional radio range

VORTAC† VOR and TACAN combination

VOT VOR airborne equipment test facility

VPA Vertical path angle

VPT Visual manoeuvre with prescribed track

VRB Variable

VSA By visual reference to the ground

VSP Vertical speed

VTF Vector to final

VTOL Vertical take-off and landing

VV . . . Vertical visibility (followed by figures in METAR/SPECI and TAF)

W

W West or western longitude

W White

W . . . Sea-surface temperature (followed by figures in METAR/SPECI)

WAAS† Wide area augmentation system

WAC. . . World Aeronautical Chart — ICAO 1:1 000 000 (followed by name/title)

WAFC World area forecast centre

WB Westbound

WBAR Wing bar lights

WDI Wind direction indicator

WDSPR Widespread

WED Wednesday

WEF With effect from or effective from

WGS-84 World Geodetic System — 1984

WI Within

WID Width or wide
WIE With immediate effect or effective immediately
WILCO† Will comply
WIND Wind
WIP Work in progress
WKN Weaken or weakening
WNW West-north-west
WO Without
WPT Way-point
WRNG Warning
WS Wind shear
WSPD Wind speed
WSW West-south-west
WT Weight
WTSPT Waterspout
WWW Worldwide web
WX Weather

X

X Cross
XBAR Crossbar (of approach lighting system)
XNG Crossing
XS Atmospherics

Y

Y Yellow
YCZ Yellow caution zone (runway lighting)
YES* Yes (affirmative) (to be used in AFS as a procedure signal)
YR Your

Z

Z Coordinated Universal Time (in meteorological messages)

----

† When radiotelephony is used, the abbreviations and terms are transmitted as spoken words.

‡ When radiotelephony is used, the abbreviations and terms are transmitted using the individual letters in non-phonetic form.

* Signal is also available for use in communicating with stations of the maritime mobile service.

Signal for use in the teletypewriter service only.

REFERENCES

https://www.wired.com/2010/09/0917selfridge-first-us-air-fatality

http://thevintageaviator.co.nz

Walsh, by Ross Ewing & Richard Williams, 2011

https://teara.govt.nz/en/1966/air-transport-and-airports/page-2

https://www.boeing.com/features/innovation-quarterly/dec2016/feature-technology-checklist.page

Flying Fortress, by Edward Jablonski, 1965

The Great Planes, by James Gilbert, 1970

Missing, by Chris Rudge, 2001

https://nzhistory.govt.nz/media/sound/craig-saxon-announces-erebus-flight-lost

"Gordon Vette", Aircraft Enthusiasts' Group. 30 July 2017.

"Commission Effects and Outcomes", The Erebus Story: the Loss of TE901. New Zealand Air Line Pilots' Association (NZALPA). 2009.

Sumwalt, Robert L. (January 25, 2011). "Investigating and Preventing Organizational Accidents" (PDF). National Transportation Safety Board.

Byrne, Evan (July 6, 2012). "FAA TV: NTSB The Human Factor". Federal Aviation Administration.

"Commission Effects and Outcomes". The Erebus Story: the Loss of TE901. New Zealand Air Line Pilots' Association (NZALPA). 2009.

Baragwanath, David (2009). "The Significant and Key Role of the Prosecutor in Upholding the Rule of Law" (PDF). Victoria Faculty of Law. Victoria University of Wellington.

"About Gordon Vette". The Erebus Story: the Loss of TE901. New Zealand Air Line Pilots' Association (NZALPA). 2009.

"Abridged Transcript of a Sundstrand, Model B Cockpit Voice Recorder, Serial No. 256: Removed from ZK-NZP (Flight TE 901) which was Involved in an Accident at Ross Island on 28 November 1979" (PDF).

The Erebus Story: the Loss of TE901. New Zealand Air Line Pilots' Association (NZALPA). 31 May 1980.

Fernando, Capt. G A (December 21, 2014). "And they called it pilot error". The Island.

Forecasts 2009 – Safety and security are in the doldrums. Flightglobal.com. 2009-01-13.

https://www.iata.org/publications/Documents/iata-annual-review-2018.pdf

ACKNOWLEDGMENTS

I wish to thank a few people who have helped me along my flying career, whether they realise it or not, our fun conversations or the serious chats we had and the discussions around flying, really helped me write this book. Thank you.

First of all I wish to mention those I met and bonded with at some stage in my life and who are no longer flying with us. May they Rest In Peace.

- Wayne Thompson 2008
- Pip Borrman 2009
- Nick Cree 2010
- Stacey Hopper 2010

As I worked through the list of all the people who have influenced my flying career, it is incredible to see the number of people who can influence just one person. Thank you.

Neville Swan (first gliding instructor)

Craig McNeal (first power flying instructor)
Aaron Shipman
Aaron 'AJ' Jeffery
Aaron Pearce
Aaron Marshall
Adam Eltham
Aiden Campbell
Alan Beck QSM
Alistair Blake
Amiria Wallis
Anastasios Raptis
Andrew Gormlie
Andrew Hope
Andrew Lorimer
Andrew Love
Andrew Sunde
Andrew Telfer
Andy Mackay
Andy Stevenson MNZM
Angelo Cruz
Ben Lee
Ben Marcus
Ben Pryor NZGM
Benjamin James
Bevan Dewes
Bill Reid
Bradley Marsh
Brett Emeny
Brett Nicholls
Bruce Lynch
Bryn Lockie
Carlo Santoro
Chantel Strooh
Charles J Cook

Chris Barry
Chris Bromley
Chris Pond
Chris Satler
Chris Sperou OAM
Christina Harvey
Christoph Berthoud
Connell Weston
Conor Neill
Cosmo Mead
Craig Piner
Craig Rook
Craig Speck
Craig Steel
Craig Walecki
Daniel Campbell
Darren Crabb
Daryl Gillett
Dave Blackwell
David Brown
Dave Campbell
Dave Cogan
Dave Hayman
Dave Rouse
David Lowy AM
David Morgan
David Saunders
David Wilkinson
Dennis Eckhoff
Derry Belcher
Desmond Barry
Don Lockie
Donovan Burns
Doug Batten

Doug Brown
Doug Burrell
Dwight Weston
Enya Mae McPherson
Eric Morgan
Eva Keim
Flo Smith
Frank Parker
Gareth Wheeler
Gavin Conroy
Gavin Trethewey
Gavin Weir
Gene De Marco
Geoff Cooper
George Oldfield JP
Giovanni Nustrini
Graeme 'Spud' Spurdle
Graham Lake
Graham Nevill
Graham Orphan
Grant Armishaw
Grant 'Muddy' Murdoch
Greg Quinn
Guy Bourke
Harvey Lockie
Hayden Leech
HH Prince Faisal bin Abdulla bin Mohammed Saud
Ian Lilley
Ian 'Iggy' Wood
Imogen Ling
James Aldridge
Jamie Wagner
Jason Alexander
Jason Haggitt DSD

Jay McIntyre
Jed Melling
Jill McCaw
Jim Rankin DSD
Jock MacLachlan
Joe Oldfield
John Duxfield ARCOM
John Gemmell
John Lamont
John Martin
John McCaw
Jonathan Bowen
Joseph D'Ath
Josh Camp
Juan Ferandoes
Jurgis Kairys
Karl Stol
Keith McKenzie QSM
Keith Skilling
Keith Stephens
Kenny Love
Kermit Weeks
Kevin Langley
Kevin Vile
Kirsty Coleman
Kishan Bhashyam
Kris Vette
Lawrence Acket
Liberio Riosa
Lionel Page
Liz King (Mother Goose)
Lloyd Galloway
Loïc Ifrah
Louisa 'Choppy' Patterson

Malcolm Clement
Martin Schulze
Mark Helliwell
Mark Lowndes
Mary Patterson
Matt Hall
Matt Ledger
Maurizio Folini
Melissa Andrzejewski (nee Pemberton)
Michael Bach
Michael Jeffs
Mike Clark
Mike Foster
Mike Harvey
Mike Jorgenson
Mike Read
Mike Slack
Nando Parrado
Nathan Graves
Nick Tarascio
Nigel Cooper
Nigel Lamb
Nina Hayman
Paul Andronicou
Paul 'Huggy' Hughan
Paul 'Simmo' Simmons AM CSM
Pete Meadows
Pete Pring Shambler
Peter Harper
Peter Jefferies
Peter Thorpe
Phil Freeman
Phill Hooker
Ray Burns

Ray Richards
Reuben Muir
Rex Pemberton
Richard Button
Richard Hectors
Richard Hood
Rev. Dr Richard Waugh QSM
Richie McCaw ONZ
Rick Watson
Rob Fox
Rob Fry
Rob Mackley
Rob Neil
Rob Owens
Rob Weavers
Robert Burns
Roy Crane
Roy Cunningham
Ruan Heynike
Ruth Nisbet
Ryan Brooks
Ryan Francis
Sam Elimelech
Scott 'Macka' McKenzie
Sean Perrett
Shaun Clark
Shaun Roseveare
Simon J Gault
Simon Lockie
Simon Mundell
Simone Moro
SQNLDR Les Munro CNZM DSO QSO DFC JP
Steve Ahrens
Steve Wallace

Stephen Boyce
Stephen Death
Steve Gibson
Steve Newland
Steve Jurd
Steven Perreau
Stu Wards
Tasos Raptis
Tee Jay Sullivan
Tim Marshall
Sir Tim Wallis
Todd O'Hara
Tracy Dixon
Wayne Fowler
Wayne Ormrod
Weston Connell
Vaughan Davis
Yoshihide 'Yoshi' Muroya

ABOUT THE AUTHOR

With a passion for aviation passed on from his father who worked in the National Airways Corporation (NAC) office in Auckland, New Zealand. Fletcher often heard about the NAC DC3 Kaimai Ranges crash, this had made an impact on his father as he knew one of the flight attendants killed in the accident.

Fletcher flew solo in a glider at the age of 16, then tried parachuting several dozen times, before graduating onto paragliding, and finally obtained his Private Pilots License. He is the producer of the global television show "FlightPathTV" which is on air in over 60 countries, and travels extensively interviewing pilots from around the world.

Coupled with twenty years of experience working with global entrepreneurs through EO (Entrepreneurs Organisation), training them to experience share between each other and to learn from any mistakes, Fletcher selected and compiled these stories to help us learn from others. To ensure current and future pilots will be safe in the skies.

ALSO BY FLETCHER MCKENZIE